THEY DID SOMETHING ABOUT IT

They Did Something About It

ROBERT M. BARTLETT

Author of
THEY DARED TO LIVE
BUILDERS OF A NEW WORLD
A BOY'S BOOK OF PRAYERS

ASSOCIATION PRESS

1943

347 Madison Avenue   New York

COPYRIGHT, 1939, BY
THE INTERNATIONAL COMMITTEE
OF YOUNG MEN'S CHRISTIAN ASSOCIATIONS

PRINTED IN THE UNITED STATES OF AMERICA

TO
MARY WARREN

PREFACE

THE ten men and women in this book represent ten professions, five nations and four races. They are very much a part of the contemporary scene; and form a stimulating cross section of our turbulent times.

They are all pioneers in some field, a progressive and challenging company of reformers. They differ in their approach to human problems, but are one in their effort to create a better world order.

These life sketches remind us that the worthy citizen in every generation lives ahead of his time. The penalty of developed men is that they must march in the vanguard. They refuse to accept conditions as they are. They will not surrender before the blunders and tyrannies of society. They do something about it.

When brutes and bombs about us give evidence of the debacle of civilization, it is heartening to discover some of our noble contemporaries. They prove that the future belongs to the years and the centuries. They renew hope that was lost for many of us in our present tragic world.

R. M. B.

CONTENTS

Preface — vii

"The World Isn't Finished":
CHARLES FRANKLIN KETTERING — 1

"The Moral Limitations of the World Must Be Charted":
RICHARD E. BYRD — 18

"I Am an Optimist":
EDOUARD BENEŠ — 34

"It Is the Struggle that Gives Value to Life":
JAWAHARLAL NEHRU — 44

"The Way of Liberty":
LOUIS DEMBITZ BRANDEIS — 61

Cotton Picker, LL.D.:
MARY McLEOD BETHUNE — 72

"Reason and Truth Are Eternally Free":
THOMAS MANN — 82

First Woman of the Orient:
MADAME CHIANG KAI-SHEK — 94

The Lure of the Impossible:
CHEVALIER JACKSON — 111

A Promise to Keep:
MARGARET SANGER — 126

Sources of Quotations — 145

THEY DID SOMETHING ABOUT IT

"The World Isn't Finished":

CHARLES FRANKLIN KETTERING

THE first money he ever earned, fourteen dollars for cutting a neighbor's wheat crop, was squandered on a telephone purchased from a mail-order house. The day of its arrival he dismantled the apparatus to study it. He was adept at dismembering his mother's sewing machine and at carving a model threshing machine out of a block of wood. This farm boy, who spent his youth in the country near Loudonville, Ohio, was a born experimenter. He did not play ball after school; he never went to the pool hall. When classes were over he could be seen trudging the five miles back to the farm, stooping forward, as if studying the ground, engrossed in his own thoughts. When he was not milking, cultivating corn, or digging potatoes, he was tinkering. Years later, while he was guest on a yacht off the Florida coast, his host asked him how he came to be known as the monkey-wrench scientist. "That's easy," Charles Franklin Kettering drawled, "I was born and spent my youth on a farm."

At nineteen he was teacher of thirty children in the one-room Bunker Hill School. He created a sensation one spring day when he dismissed school and took the children to Loudonville to see an x-ray machine that had arrived in a railway exhibition car. He examined the coils, the wires, and tubes with curious eyes; and explained its marvels to the pupils. But the unconventional visit stirred up a tumult of criticism. The teacher was hired to teach the three R's and not to fill the heads of youth with fantastic ideas. He almost lost his job.

That summer Charles went to Wooster Normal School to study Greek in preparation for college. There he heard of Ohio State University and its courses in electrical engineering. It was exactly what he wanted. He would go to Columbus in the fall! A few hours later he was carried home with a terrific, puzzling headache. The doctor thought it might be brain fever brought about by overstudy. For days he sat with cold packs on his eyes, threatened with loss of eyesight.

The dream of the State University was definitely sidetracked. He found himself in the village of Mifflin, teaching older children in the top-floor room. The local druggist became his friend. Together in the back of the drug store they would experiment at night with photography and electricity. Determined to become an engineer, he kept on struggling to make his dream come true. He was twenty-two when he reached the University with thirty-five dollars in his pocket.

He forgot about his weak eyes and lost himself in the scientific laboratories. Curiosity impelled him. There were a thousand secrets to unravel. In the spring the headaches renewed their torture and he collapsed with something like a stroke. They carried him home half blind. Bitterly disappointed over his failure, he rested for a few weeks and then got a job with the telephone gang digging post holes. His ingenious mind was active figuring how to set the poles uniformly on hills and in hollows, where hitherto they had been planted hit and miss. Before long he was made foreman. The outdoor life helped his eyes and he was able to read again.

When he returned to the University for his sophomore year he was twenty-five, still poor, and forced to earn his own expenses. A Columbus factory had trouble keeping up steam in its boiler. The experts were called in but they did not solve the problem. The manager heard of the handy student-repair-man and sent for Kettering. He had to pull hard at the boiler room door to open it. Sending the fireman home for lunch, he pushed up a window and pried open the door; and soon was watching a blazing fire. The draft did the trick. He knew enough physics to build a fire.

He was called in as consultant on a telephone cable line south of Columbus. The company experts and the university faculty were unable to spot the trouble; then someone thought of Kettering. When he got out to the bad cable line the telephone superintendent said:

"We'll pay you twenty-five dollars if you'll spot it. Wait. We'll make it fifty if you'll find it by tomorrow."

Kettering, like the countryman he has never yet ceased being, looked at the superintendent. Would they make it a hundred dollars if he found it by morning? They said they would, considering it absolutely impossible.

His arm throbbed from a recent vaccination; he had fever; but he got busy hooking up his batteries, galvanometer, and resistance box, making a Wheatstone's bridge with the cable line. Then he waited. They taught the theory of the Wheatstone's bridge at the University. You learned that, if you hooked up a galvanometer between two wires of a parallel circuit, no current would flow if both wires had equal potential; but that had absolutely nothing to do with spotting a fault in a defective cable with the subscribers shouting for service. It got darker, colder, and still he waited.

They taught you in school that if you put current from a battery over a wet wire, the current flowing through the wire would put a film of hydrogen bubbles around it, polarizing it, insulating it. With it getting later and colder, Kettering made that hook-up. He waited again. Feeling sicker, he kept waiting until after midnight, until the temperature of that cable stopped changing from the warmth of day to the cold of night. Then he started testing.

He forgot his throbbing arm as he threw in the switch of his battery to make a good wire out of a defective one with a film of hydrogen bubbles for a little while—just long enough for him to flip his switch over to make the Wheatstone-bridge circuit, to balance it, and to take his readings. It was a simple business of his, calculating ratios between resistances. He found the break to be where his lonely midnight science said it was; he found it by sticking his jackknife into a splice where a little bullet hole near the splice had let in water. And he got his hundred dollars.

Now, they asked, could he splice in a new piece of cable? They'd give him twenty-five dollars more. Kettering beamed through his thick glasses at the superintendent. Would they make it fifty if he made the splice in one day?

Why, that was impossible. He'd have to test out each wire of all that tangle of wires, ringing out, as they say, wire by wire. They agreed to make it fifty.

So now they watched him, not having slept all night, working all this day. They saw his nimble, strong hands testing out just one wire and then joining the others in rotation round the cable. He'd learned it at Ashland that time the splicing experts hadn't come from Cleveland, and he'd finally said, "Come on, boys! We'll do it!" With an ordinary plumber and lineman, he'd worked that whole week-end with no sleep, learning it.

That night he returned to the campus with one hundred and fifty dollars in his pocket.

After graduating at the University he was employed by the National Cash Register Company to invent a way to run cash registers by electricity. It was said to be an impossible undertaking, but he shut himself up in the workshop to perfect a start-stop motor. He succeeded, and the new product brought a boom to the factory. The old handcrank machines became obsolete.

He realized the capacity of the inventor to create dissatisfaction among purchasers. He spent his spare time with the sales force gleaning their ideas of what people wanted. His pockets were bulging with sketches for new experiments. There was always work to do at home after his long hours in the laboratory. Once in a while Mrs. Kettering would succeed in enticing him to go to a theater. But his program would usually be covered with drawings of new projects that he must tackle the next day.

The eccentric management dismissed him after he had contributed brilliant inventions that brought millions in profits. In 1909 he was working in the barn of a friend, calling himself manager of the Dayton Engineering Laboratories Company, which was later to be called the Delco Company. Mrs. Kettering's savings of $1,500 bought a lathe for the shop. This barn laboratory launched into big problems, such as electric ignition for automobiles. The Cadillac Motor Car Company were disgusted with their ignition system. A set of dry batteries would last only two hundred miles; and magneto ignition had proved impossible. Boss Ket, as he was called by his shop assistants, was determined to conquer the impossible again. He perfected a dry battery good for two thousand miles, but there was baffling trouble with the coils that caused him to toil through long days and to toss through sleepless nights. Mrs. Kettering put in another $1,500 that she had saved from her music teaching into a new universal milling machine to help the struggling shop. Back and forth he shuttled to Detroit and Chicago, trying to aid the manufacturers in perfecting his idea.

One night as he lay in bed a flash of revelation solved the coil problem. He switched the two wires leading from the dry batteries so that the negative instead of the positive led to the contact point. He had found the secret! No sooner was this problem straightened out than he was summoned back to a puzzle caused by the relays in the Delco ignition system. The problem seemed insurmountable. After futile hours in the factory the tired inventor started for Dayton. That night in his Pullman berth he reached in the dark for one of the relays. He began feeling the pole pieces and the armature. The poles were rounded instead of flat. That would concentrate the magnetism, holding the armature tighter against the pole piece than it should. The next morning he explained his solution to the Cadillac factory and the Delco ignition system was complete.

One day he told the president of the Cadillac Company that he believed he could perfect an electric starter for cars. The president regaled him with stories of innumerable broken arms, and of motorists crushed to death against the walls of their garages because they made the mistake of cranking their cars when in gear. A close friend of the president had died of a broken jaw sustained when he gallantly offered to crank the stalled motor of a lady who was blocking traffic on the Belle Isle Bridge. On the train that night Kettering outlined his new invention. He perfected his starter and tested it in a factory model. Shortly afterward he drove his car into a ditch and was laid up with a broken leg. The Cadillac factory wired that their one and only model had been burned. He set out for the factory with his leg in a plaster cast and spent the day under the ruined automobile until he got the starter in order.

"The price of progress is trouble," he is fond of saying in his homely philosophic manner. In 1913 he turned to the study of automobile fuel. People wanted faster and more powerful cars. There was no room for larger motors, and, when he tried to get more power out of them by increasing the compression in the cylinder, the engines knocked. "We began by looking at the flame of exploding gas through a quartz window set in an engine cylinder. When the knock occurred, we discovered that the flame was yellowish or orange, but there was no knock when the flame was blue. We did not know much even then, and we do not now, but we knew enough to try the effect of a change of color. We put a stain in the gasoline. What we used was iodine. That changed the color both of the gasoline and of the flame in the engine, and it stopped the knock. Don't ask me why; I don't know the answer—yet. But iodine was too expensive, too scarce, so we hunted for something else. We tried a lot of chemicals in succession, hunting for one that was effective—and cheap. One substance we tried spoiled the spark plugs and another gave off a foul odor, but our search was growing warmer because all the effective substances were compounds of next-door neighbors in the table of elements. Inevitably we were led to try the lead compound that is offered today at practically every filling station in the land either as lead-treated regular gasoline or as ethyl gasoline. It is now used in 75 per cent of all the gasoline sold in filling stations."

There is a story that he likes to tell that illustrates his willingness to tackle any problem that confronts him: "I was making a motor trip down in Kentucky, running some tests, and had gone far off the road. The map didn't show any roads leading away from the place, it was so small. It was late in the afternoon and I wanted to get back home before dark. Driving along, I came upon a little stream bed which was the only road there was. There I overtook an old gentleman driving a donkey hooked to a stone boat loaded with milk cans. I said, 'Neighbor, what is the best way to go to Cincinnati from here?' And he said, 'Go right up to the forks in the road. Now, it don't make much difference which fork you take but, to tell you the truth, stranger, if I was going to Cincinnati I wouldn't start from here.' I think we sometimes get to thinking like the old Kentuckian. But we have to recognize that, whatever our destination, we must start from *here*."

Mr. Kettering set up an endowment in Dayton to pay a first-class medical research man to keep in touch with new developments and to pass on information to the Dayton doctors in weekly meetings. Results led to a number of valuable contributions, such as the artificial fever machine. "With this machine we can give you a fever," he explains. "We can give you one hundred and six degrees for five hours. When we first started that, a patient had to spend three or four days in a hospital after a treatment. Everybody said that was right, a natural weakness resulting from fever. But we kept hunting around, and found it was not natural weakness. It was found that the patient sweated all the salt out of his body. So we gave the patient salt water the next time. After the treatment he got into his car and drove home." The fever machine is now used in many hospitals and has proved helpful in treating a number of diseases. The inventor says, "Incurable diseases are only those the doctors don't know how to cure."

Mr. Kettering is a typical mid-westerner, plain spoken, droll, a born handy man and teacher. Tall, somewhat stooped, he will look at you in his straightforward way, bright eyes peering through thick spectacles. He impresses you with his unshakable faith in the future. And man's ingenuity holds the key to this future.

"A research problem is not solved by apparatus; it is solved in a man's head," as he puts it. "Some business men believe that if you build a beautiful laboratory, and fill it with expensive equipment, and hire a number of high-salaried men with lots of scientific degrees, you will have a fine research organization.

"Maybe. But it reminds me of the artist who decided to be like Michelangelo. So he spent years studying every detail of the great artist's life. He got himself the same kind of studio, the same paints, brushes, canvas and clothes. Then he settled down to paint. 'I can't understand,' he said, 'why the pictures I turn out are so rotten.'

"No. Facilities are all right in a laboratory. But it's the men that count—just as in a studio it is the artist who counts. And the good research man, by the way, is an artist. Work in a laboratory may be weeks and months of drudgery. Some of that can be done by ordinary workers. But when you break through into new territory, enter an unknown door, go down that lonesome road, it is the artist's power of creative imagination which carries you.

"If research men haven't got the inner spark, the curiosity, the wonder, the *feel* of things, they are no good. A good research man never says, 'It can't be done'; he says, 'It hasn't been done yet.'"

Change is inevitable and wholesome for all concerned, he insists. "Just the minute you get satisfied with what you've got, the concrete has begun to set in your head. Research is an organized method for keeping you reasonably dissatisfied with what you have.

"A research laboratory is trying to improve methods, improve products, branch out in new directions. And one thing you learn in such a laboratory is how fast these changes are coming, how swiftly the frontiers of our knowledge are being extended.

"Change seems slow, but it is so fast that any big manufacturing company, however prosperous, which keeps on doing things as it is doing them now will be in trouble very shortly. The present motorcars seem close to perfection, as they have every year since 1905. But any company which does not greatly improve its cars in the next five years will find itself in the hands of a receiver. No business of any kind can keep on indefinitely doing what it is doing now. It must change or go under. And that applies in a general way to individuals also.

"That is why my favorite definition of research is this: 'Trying to find out what you are going to do when you can't keep on doing what you are doing now.'

"In research we need a lot of intelligent ignorance. Whenever you begin to think you know all about any subject, it stops your progress dead in that subject. As the old colored fellow said: 'It ain't the things you *don't* know that hurts you. It's the things you *think* you know for sure that ain't so.' The electrical people, thirty years ago, *knew* that you couldn't develop an electrical self-starter. That was my good luck."

He told how in the early days of the closed motor cars it took seventeen days to paint a car. He arranged a conference. Painters thought they could reduce the time to fifteen days. He was not satisfied. He went into a New York shop and bought a lacquer tray, inquired where it was made, and went to New Jersey to see the manufacturer. The answer was found in less than two years' time. A lacquer finish was perfected that could be applied to a car in a few minutes, a finish more durable than any previously known.

"The chief thing we ought to do is quit being afraid of the future," he explained. "Change is the law of life. We should work *with* change instead of being forced into it. If you refuse to change, if you just sit down and rest, the best place to sit down is in front of the undertaker's office."

Mr. Kettering believes that the inventive capacity of men can lead us out of our present economic depression.

"A great many people think engineering and scientific development have got ahead of our social-absorption ability," he writes. "I wish that we would look at it in a different way. A man in very great haste to get to a destination came to a railway station, the train was due to leave at eleven o'clock, but he found to his great consternation when he had got there that it had left at ten o'clock. He sued the railroad company because he said they had pulled out an hour ahead of time. They were brought to trial; the railroad company testified that they did not pull out ahead of time; that was the train of the day before and they were twenty-three hours late.

"I think that may be the reason that we think engineering is ahead—it is a lap behind.

"There's an old story about a fellow who was walking along the road on his way to church. He was all shined up, with his best clothes and new shoes, because he was going to pass the collection box.

"He went by a deep mudhole, and heard a poor frog croaking for help. 'Please help me out,' said the frog. 'I'm down here, I haven't had a thing to eat for three days, and I'm going to die.'

"Well, the church-goer was a sympathetic soul, but he allowed he would have to do a lot of explaining if he passed the collection box in muddy clothes. So he said, 'Now I tell you, frog, if you will wait until church is out, I will put on some old clothes and come to help you. That's the best I can do for you.'

"So after church he was hurrying home to change his clothes, when he saw a frog hopping along the road. He said, 'Hello! Aren't you the frog that was in the mudhole?'

" 'Yes,' said the frog.

" 'Well,' said the man, 'who helped you out?'

"The frog said, 'Nobody. I got out myself.'

" 'But you told me,' said the man, 'that you had been trying to get out for three days and couldn't make it, and you were getting weaker from hunger all the time.'

" 'Yes,' said the frog, 'but after you left a snake started to come after me.'

"Many a business man is like that frog. When the old snake, the sheriff, starts after him, he learns he wasn't half trying before. The sheriff makes him think, makes him discard old methods, opens up his mind. A great apostle of open-mindedness, the sheriff. We have had more open-mindedness in this country since 1929 than I ever saw before in my life."

In 1936 Charles Kettering received the Washington Award presented by the Western Society of Engineers "in recognition of devoted, unselfish, and pre-eminent service in advancing human progress." In his address, *Research and Social Progress*, he said, "In the development of any new industry, it doesn't come full blown. It doesn't come as a completed entity. In fact, I doubt whether anybody is ever conscious of creating an industry at the time it is started. Certainly I know that Oersted didn't know he was creating an industry when he held an electric wire over a compass needle and found it was deflecting. He had searched for that for a long while. Michael Faraday came a little bit farther and wound a coil. Our own Joseph Henry, in this country, was a contemporary in the development of the magnet. But in that simple process of winding a coil on a bar of iron the fundamental principle of the telegraph was developed, and our Morse, taking that as a clue, succeeded in developing the principles, over a very short distance, of our present telegraph. But then these elementary principles and the enormous communication system that we have today in the handling of the printed telegram represented millions of dollars of expended money, heartaches, hundreds of thousands of hours, disappointments, discouragements, and everything else. Between the elementary principle and the finished commercial product comes the great work field in which industry has made its progress.

"Alexander Graham Bell, trying to improve the telegraph, trying to facilitate the methods of sending messages, discovered the principles of the telephone, and out of that came another new industry that employs thousands of men, and puts much money to work. This industry was developed; nobody thinking at the time that it was started that what Bell had discovered represented the basic principle of the new industry. Out of that and other important developments came the principles of radio and other unthought of, and undreamed of, things.

"We can send a message to the farthest point of the earth in a fourteenth of a second, but it may take years before it gets from the outside of a man's head to the inside.

"We sometimes fool ourselves by saying that we know a great deal scientifically. We do not know how to operate some of the factors to our benefit. We have been able, especially in sanitation and medicine, to improve human welfare and living conditions tremendously. We have in many other of the mechanical arts been able to do many things which people want. I think the best way to evaluate those things is to try to turn time backwards; in other words, let's see, if we didn't have this or that, what would we do? I happened to be talking to a friend of mine the other day who was making a trip in an automobile from Detroit to Miami, Florida. It was the celebration of the twenty-fifth anniversary of a similar trip he had made. Twenty-five years ago there wasn't a single mile of paved road between Detroit and Jacksonville, to say nothing of how few in Miami. All the pavements we had were in the towns and now most of the pavements are in the country.

"We have forgotten that in that twenty-five years the enormous development of the motor car as a leader in industry has produced an almost complete change in our method of living. It isn't the automobile from a manufacturing standpoint that is represented by that industry. Some thirty-odd years ago I had a canvass made of the number of people employed in the motor car industry. The best figures I could get were about one thousand people. The best figures that we have today are eleven million people directly or indirectly sustained by that industry. The motor car industry is everything that goes with it. It is the highway, the steel, glass, rubber, petroleum. You can't tell what an idea is going to be. You can't tell what its future is going to lead to.

"I do not feel that anybody should be discouraged and never have, because out of all these experiences it is impossible for us, even those in industry, to project industrial developments a few years ahead. . . . People say, 'What are the next great industries?' You can't tell what they are because you don't know when an industry is starting. You can't tell what is going to come because, as long as some of the factors are not there, it doesn't develop. The radio became an industry almost overnight.

"We have in the past few decades become too expert in bookkeeping. We begin to think of return on capital, and yet not every motive of our life depends upon return on capital. When you buy a dining room table, do you try to figure out what the earning on that is going to be, what per cent you get on your invested capital? When you send your boy or girl to school do you try to figure a net return on that? I sometimes think that, if we tried to raise human children on the same basis as that of the highly organized bookkeeping system upon which we are trying to raise industrial children, a baby nine months old would have to be earning its living.

"Mr. Dunlop didn't develop the tire for motor cars. His son rode to school over a piece of rough pavement on a solid rubber-tired bicycle and he complained about it. His father, who was a veterinarian, said, 'I think I can fix it.' He made a wooden wheel and on the edges of the wheel he tacked a canvas loop. Inside of that he put a rubber tube and with a football pump he pumped it up. That was the first pneumatic tire, conceived not as a scientific invention, but something to please a small boy.

"If you read the discussions in the scientific papers of the years in which the pneumatic tire was making its way on racing bicycles—because that was the only use of it—you will find very learned discussions among engineers as to the whys and wherefores, why it wouldn't work and why it would work. No progress was made until a very much unknown bicycle rider defeated the champion and then everybody said, 'There must be something in it.' In other words, Mr. Dunlop produced a sample, a working sample. I sometimes think we discuss too much and don't make enough samples whereby we can get the thing across. I am a great believer in all the formulas and other things that necessarily are used in engineering, but I feel that the fact is very much better ahead of the formula than behind it.

"If you go back and trace the history of all industry, you will find that exact thing. Somebody did something that everybody was sure wouldn't work. It wouldn't work under certain conditions but the fellow who succeeded didn't do it under those conditions. He did it under slightly different conditions. Out at the Rosenwald Museum we saw the story of the development of power, with a replica of Watt's old engine. It was interesting, but how many of the things that were there could you argue out if somebody hadn't tried the experiment?"

He enjoys pointing out the success of an innovation such as the Diesel engine, and prophesies far greater achievement in this field. Air conditioning is bound to come in our public buildings and our homes. By 1950 people will no more be willing to live in a 1937 house than they are willing today to drive a 1925 model car. Over fourteen million

Americans are employed today in seven new industries, and there are more new industries yet to be developed.

This amazing inventor keeps his eyes focused on the future. He refuses to lose faith in man. He believes in progress and in the blessings that tomorrow will bring. "All the rest of your lives are going to be lived in the future," he argues, "unless you spend too much time wishing you had lived them in the past. Therefore, I would like to make that future just about as nice a place to live in as I can think of. If you don't carry over too much of the old, dirty past there; if you begin to think of a polished, bright, and glistening and glorious future and say, 'Why is it, it can't be that way?' you can solve those problems, because I think you can make them anything you want.

"We have a lot of things that we ought to tear down and throw away. I say we ought to rebuild this country. The first thing you know, the bankers and economists will say, 'Where are you going to get the money from?' I am going to tell you where we are going to get it. In exactly the same place we got the money to build it this far. We didn't have any to start with. All we did was dig this building out of the ground and put it up here. It didn't have to grow. It has always been here, but it wasn't in this particular shape.

"The wealth of the nation is not in dollars; it is in useful material, and the positive side of economics is the movement of useful materials through the channel of trade. That must always go ahead of the return flow of money through the counting house.

"What are some of the things we would like to have? Why can't we have them? Research is not a thing that goes with a laboratory. It is purely a principle and anybody can apply it. It is simply to try to find out if you are satisfied with what you have got, where you are and what you are doing. Write down ten things that you don't like about your business, about yourself, or the things you are doing or working with as your problems. You may not be able to solve the number one, because it may be a very difficult thing, but you will be able to pick out one of them, just as you put the word in the cross-word puzzle. Finally, after a period of time you will be surprised to find out how these things break down if you persistently work at them.

"I think the next ten years is going to see a complete renaissance in engineering and scientific development. It is all ahead of us. Every period in time has always had somebody say: 'I don't see what new there is to be done.' Go out and look. Take any book that gives you the history of industry, and tear out half of the book; read up to that, and they will say you have finished. If we can take out 'Your world is finished,' and put instead 'The world is begun,' we have a marvelous place to live and a marvelous future ahead of us.

"However large our troubles may loom, from time to time, nothing can stop the progress of this country." The resourceful scientist does not imply that progress is automatic. Man must strive and do his part. Man must believe, experiment, and reach onward! Everyone who contributes to his own day must live a little ahead of the crowd. "The man who has the greatest foresight is the man who is out of step at the present time."

"The world isn't finished!"

"*The Moral Limitations of the
World Must Be Charted*":

RICHARD E. BYRD

RICHARD E. BYRD's career of adventure began in his fourteenth year, when he made a trip alone around the world. A family friend invited him to visit the Philippine Islands. While attending court where his host, Judge Carson, presided, he was fascinated by the *punkahs*, the large palm leaf fans that were manipulated by a servant to keep off the flies and to create a breeze. He prevailed upon the servant to let him work the fan; and did it so vigorously that plaster was knocked off the ceiling upon the head of the judge. The jurist indignantly demanded the arrest of the unseen offender. Dick fled, pursued by the native bailiff, who captured him and led him back. The judge was surprised to discover who the offender was, but solemnly declared a fine. The culprit paid from money in his pocket that had been given him by the judge to bring him to the Islands.

On another occasion he joined the constabulary in their investigation of an insurrection and rode to an inland village. He rode ahead of the party and found himself in a hamlet of the rebels. They tried to persuade him to stay with them. He clutched at his revolver, and turned his pony back toward the troopers he had lost. "Suddenly, as I was approaching a small stream," he later described it, "several *ladrones* [highwaymen], with bolos in their hands heavy enough to cut through a body twice as big as mine, jumped out at me from the bush. They swept their heavy blades around me and I whipped up my pony, heading for the river and completely forgetting my pistol. They followed, but after I got through the water they never had a chance to catch me. I never stopped until I found the detachment, where I was soundly scolded for my rashness. I agreed with everything that was said, particularly as I had been almost fired upon by the advance guard as I raced forward at a gallop."

Later, on Darim Island, he tried to doctor a sick soldier, who died in a few hours of cholera. That night he was sure that he was going to die. He imagined that he had pains in his stomach and spent the night writing farewell letters to his family. He was quarantined a hundred yards from camp. During these days he could hear the groans of men dying in the huts. Cut off from the world, they were forced to live on parrots and monkeys. It was a sobering experience.

He set out for Ceylon and the Red Sea on a British tramp steamer. The second mate had teased him for being an American and he was glad when the officer forgot to wind the chronometer and they got off their course. They steered west until they hit Madagascar and then piloted up the coast to Port Said. It was a memorable lesson in navigation.

On his return, this son of a distinguished Virginia family entered Virginia Military Institute. Richard was not big and brawny, but he liked athletics and determined to play football. As a result he broke a bone in his foot. This injury was to have far-reaching effects later in his life. Four years followed at the Naval Academy in Annapolis, where he made a commendable record. During his senior year, when he was captain of the gym team, he fell from the flying rings while trying to execute a difficult feat known as "dislocating," and broke the ankle of the foot that had already given him trouble.

He went about his duties, determined that he would master this handicap. "The bony knot on the outer side of my right ankle was still in two pieces," he wrote. "It clicked when I walked. Someone told me if I walked a lot I would grate the fragments together and induce a flow of osseous fluid. I did this for weeks. It hurt; but it apparently worked. I had to take my semi-annual examinations and my final examinations at the same time. After a great struggle I managed to graduate. The struggle I had made to graduate taught me a great lesson—that it is by struggle that we progress. I learned concentration during that time I had never thought I possessed."

In 1912 he received his commission and spent four years as an officer in the Navy. One day at the head of a steep gangway his ankle collapsed and he fell ten feet to land on his weak foot. In the hospital surgeons decided to hold the troublesome bone with a silver nail. But the experiment was a failure, the doctors concluded, as they saw their patient limp gamely back to his duties. There was no place for a limping officer in the navy, no matter how capable he might be. In the spring of 1916 Richard Byrd was placed on the retired list.

For several years he had been convinced that the way of escape from a life of inaction was to learn to fly. But the doctors shook their heads, "No, not with that leg." The impatient young officer wanted to shout back at them, "But you don't fly with your legs!" He did no shouting; nevertheless he was thinking all the time that he was nothing but a glorified clerk when he had been trained for more daring things, for fighting the winds and the seas. He lost twenty-five pounds through worry.

Breaking with the past, he entered the Naval Flying School in Pensacola, Florida. The joy of flying furnished a tonic that strengthened him at once. He soon became an expert flyer. During the World War he became one of the first teachers of aviation and served as chief of the American air forces in Canada.

Ever since 1917 Richard Byrd had urged a trans-Atlantic flight by American planes. He helped Lieutenant Commander Read prepare for his successful crossing, although he himself was not permitted to go. The Navy gave him permission to fly the plane C-5 across, but the craft was totally destroyed in a storm that swept the seaboard. This reverse did not hinder his zeal. He urged the Navy to try a dirigible flight, and tried to persuade Congress to establish a Naval Bureau of Aeronautics. At length the Navy informed him that he might go to England and help bring back the British dirigible ZR-3. On a trial cruise the ZR-3 burst into flames and plunged into the Humber River, losing forty-five of the forty-nine men aboard. Instead of flying the Atlantic, he had the sad task of recovering the bodies of shipmates. He returned to the United States, checked by another defeat.

In 1924 he was assigned to the dirigible Shenandoah, to fly over the North Pole. This dirigible also met with disaster at Lakewood, New Jersey. It was the third time in five years that his plans had been frustrated. For ten years he had been studying and preparing himself for the opportunity that he believed was awaiting him. He now turned to the polar regions. When he was twelve he declared that he would be the first man to reach the North Pole. He cherished the ambition to become a polar explorer. It was a rigorous goal because he came from a family who had lived for generations in the South. He disliked cold weather and was susceptible to the cold. But he toughened himself by going through the winters without an overcoat and wearing only light underwear.

In 1925 his dream of reaching the polar regions began to materialize. With Captain Bob Bartlett he organized an expedition for aerial exploration in North Greenland. He believed he could demonstrate the value of heavier-than-air machines in the field of polar exploration. He flew twenty-five hundred miles over the Greenland Ice Cap. A year later he sailed for Kings Bay, Spitzbergen, from which he and Floyd Bennett flew in their Fokker plane across the

North Pole and back to their base in less than sixteen hours. Commodore Peary and Matt Henson had reached the pole just twenty years before, having been out of contact with civilization for four hundred and twenty-nine days. The new conqueror of the North Pole was back in New York six weeks after his achievement, receiving the acclaim of the nation.

Byrd had proved what the dreamer could do. A vision cherished through the years had through discipline and scientific preparation at last come true. He had not stumbled onto achievement in any haphazard fashion; he had won his way through great odds. As he flew over the North Pole, he was just a dot in the center of ten thousand square miles of visible desolation. He felt "no larger than a pinpoint and as lonely as the tomb; as remote and detached as a star." His sentiments on this momentous day form a striking record: "I thought of the infinitesimal proportions of mortal man, of the frailty of the atoms that occupy the spaces, of the limitations of those who have taken over the conduct of civilization. I caught for the first time, as in a flash of understanding, the inadequate results of the effort to solve not only the enigmas of space and duration but the problems of mankind.

"At any point of the earth's circumference, at a given elevation, human vision encounters its limitations. The telescope amplifies a definite point, but the whole field of visibility, discernible to human eyes, is comparatively restricted. Beneath me lay a vast, silent, unoccupied field of snow and ice, varying in tone but without life. My knowledge of what existed beyond at every degree of the circle, plus my imagination, carried me into the temperate and tropic zones, the peopled spaces, the seats of empire, the scenes of turmoil, and conquest, and the survival of the fittest. I saw armies and navies beyond the fringe of that

Arctic wilderness, over which a metal mechanism made by man was plunging onward.

"I thought of the beginnings; the primitive past, the gradual development of man, the widely separated units that preyed upon one another, the readjustments that took place and of which no records remain. At that time the passing of one group or another was of small significance, in no wise affecting the world as a whole. The little peoples were too far apart to feel the consequences of the minor obligations. Slowly, out of the chaos, the units became interdependent, the races began to unite, the responsibilities of each increasing as the mutual interests expanded. Figuratively, the world became smaller and the sword longer. Each unit began to feel the effects of conflict. The gaps between the countries disappeared; the strong came to the weak and possessed them. Foreign armies conquered other lands. Flames were visible across the seas.

"War, destruction, hatred took the saddle at the peak of civilization. Today a shot fired in any country is not only heard but felt around the world. The distant tread of soldiers shakes the whole globe, saps the vitality of every nation.

"We have come through the ages worshiping in our different ways the Supreme Being that best suits our multiplied faiths, but the sum total of our occupation on this shrinking planet is a pitiful demonstration of weakness. It is not the geographical but the moral limitations of the world that must be charted and the really great explorers will be those who find the way to universal reconstruction, the first step in which is the abolition of war and the needless destruction of human life.

"These are the thoughts that occupied my mind when I flew over the North Pole and on the way back to my native land."

Three months after his return from the pole he planned to try for the twenty-five-thousand-dollar prize that Raymond Orteig offered to the flyer who made the first nonstop journey from New York to Paris. While he was preparing his plane, *America*, Charles Lindbergh made his epochal crossing and won the prize. Byrd and his three companions followed to the shores of France and demonstrated for the first time how valuable the radio could be in aviation.

Soon afterward the explorer Amundsen asked him, "Well, Byrd, what will it be now?" He answered, "The South Pole."

"A big job," said Amundsen, "but it can be done. You have the right idea. The older order is changing. Aircraft is the new vehicle for exploration. It is the only machine that can beat the Antarctic. Look here!" And he began to plan; he talked soberly and gravely, as if the fatigue and the buffetings of his magnificent journey to the South Pole (1911-1912) were still on him, and naturally his advice was good. He suggested several capable Norwegian men; he offered the use of some of his equipment; he suggested the ship—the *Samson*, which Byrd bought and renamed the *City of New York*.

He warned his American friend to look to his men: "Men are the doubtful quantities in the Antarctic. The most thorough kind of preparation, the shrewdest plan, can be destroyed by an incompetent or worthless man."

The Antarctic expedition was planned to be more than an aerial dash to the South Pole; it was a scientific expedition involving forty-two men and many projects. Hundreds of thousands of dollars had to be raised to purchase two boats, three planes, ninety-five sled dogs, building material for the entire village of Little America, and food, clothing, fuel, drugs, and the innumerable articles necessary to carry this company of men through a three-year period. At the close of 1928 the expedition reached the Bay of Whales. The building and organization of Little America was completed before winter night set in. The planes were stored in snow hangars and the men and dogs burrowed beneath the snow drifts for their long hibernation.

With spring came Byrd's successful flight with three companions to the Pole. In nineteen hours they completed a journey which had taken Amundsen fifty-three days. On November 29, 1929, Admiral Byrd wrote in his diary: "Well, it's done. We have seen the Pole and the American flag has been advanced to the South Pole. McKinley, Balchen, and June have delivered the goods. They took the Pole in their stride, neatly, expeditiously, and undismayed. If I had searched the world over I doubt if I could have found a better team. Theirs was the actual doing. But there is not a man in camp who did not assist in the preparations for the flight. Whatever merit accrues to the accomplishment must be shared with them. They are splendid."

In February the expedition turned away from Little America for the homeward journey. Much had been achieved, but the leader realized that it was only the beginning. He wrote, "The Antarctic has not been conquered. At best we simply tore away a bit more of the veil which conceals its secrets. An immense job yet remains to be done. The Antarctic will yield to no single expedition, nor yet to a dozen. In its larger aspects it still remains, and will probably remain for many years to come, one of the *undone* tasks of the world."

Problems of large geographic and scientific importance remaining to be investigated led to the organization of the Second Antarctic Expedition; and four years later Admiral Byrd was digging through the snow to the deserted village of Little America. It had been an almost superhuman task to raise funds and acquire equipment to fit out this million-dollar concern and land the winter party of fifty-six once again at this southernmost human settlement. As they entered the mess hall the telephone rang. "If Haile Selassie had crawled out from under one of the bunks, we couldn't have been more taken back," the leader records. "Nobody moved for a second.

"'Did somebody miss the boat?' asked George Noville with raised eyebrows. Peterson had found the telephone and pressed the buzzer. We heard him laugh. Poulter answered in the Ad. Building.

"'By yimminy,' said Pete, 'she works!' Then Peterson flipped a switch. The lights went on. There was a dim, faint glow in the bulbs as if registering welcome to the new arrivals."

Once again the colony was re-established in the world of ice, a peculiar settlement of scientists all absorbed in some particular specialty—geology, meteorology, astronomy, zoology, biology, aviation, radio. Dug in for the winter amid their ice-covered habitations and dark snow tunnels, they formed a beehive of activity, workshops and laboratories going full blast. Admiral Byrd had determined to carry out a strange experiment. An advance weather base should be established south of Little America and observations recorded. Realizing the difficulty of two men living together in such a place and the hazards involved, he delegated himself for the undertaking.

Bolling Advance Weather Base was built one hundred and twenty-three miles from camp. "It lay near the heart of the Ross Shelf Ice, which itself is one of the grand natural wonders of the world, a vast sheet of ice rolling from the Ross Sea to the foot of the Queen Maud Range, four hundred miles broad and upwards of six hundred feet in thickness. Where the Base was, no life had moved, nothing stirred, for centuries; the Ice Age was in complete mastery."

The shack measured nine by thirteen by eight feet. The stove was a makeshift, an ordinary caboose stove into which an oil burner had been fitted. Several lengths of stove pipe were lost in the journey, and rough joints were made from empty fuel tins. One tunnel led to a cache of food and a gasoline generator that supplied power for the radio set, another to the fuel drums, and a third served as an escape tunnel to use as an emergency exit if blizzards buried the trap door of the shack. Meteorological and auroral observations to be kept each day included: a continuous mechanical registration of barometric pressure, temperature, wind direction and velocity; twice daily visual observations of cloudiness and the state of the weather; twice daily readings of maximum and minimum thermometers in the instrument shelter topside; and twice daily visual observations of the barometer. The four instruments exacted constant attention. In addition he stood four or five auroral watches daily whenever the sky was clear enough for such displays.

From the day that Admiral Byrd began his isolation on March twenty-eighth he kept up frequent radio communication with Little America, until fumes from the stove poisoned him. He suffered acute headaches and nausea. At times he was unable to eat and too weak to move. He would lie in the lonely shack with the blizzards howling above him, his fire out and the temperature dropping to forty degrees below zero. His main radio set broke down. A coupling on the gasoline-driven generator sheared off and disabled it. He was compelled to fall back upon the emergency set, which was operated by hand-cranking. Many days he did not have the strength to turn the crank. On May thirty-first the gas fumes from the gasoline-driven generator in the food tunnel overwhelmed him and he lay in the icy darkness on the edge of death. He managed to keep himself alive through June and through the icy hell of July, when twenty-five times the thermometer crossed fifty degrees below zero, four times it passed seventy degrees, and once it stood at eighty degrees below. He kept up a semblance of communication, refusing to report his condition, because he did not want his comrades to risk their lives in an effort to break through the Antarctic night.

One day in his paralyzing weakness and pain he realized that his physical power was exhausted. Something more was necessary if he was to endure—the will to meet these testings. "That must come from deep inside me," he wrote in his diary. "But how? By taking control of my thoughts and dwelling only on those which would make for peace. A discordant mind, black with confusion and despair, would finish me off as thoroughly as the cold.

"That evening I made a desperate effort to fill my mind with the fine and comforting things of life. I surrounded myself with my family and friends; I projected myself into the sunlight, into the midst of green, growing things. I thought of all I would do when I got home; and a thousand matters which had never been more than casual now became surpassingly attractive and important. Ultimately, disorder left my mind, and when I blew out the candle I was living in a simple, uncomplicated world made up of people who wished each other well, who were peaceful and easy-going and kind."

The peace that came to him proved to be a turning point in his illness. Meanwhile, the suspicion of the men at Little America was aroused. On July nineteenth a tractor expedition set out for the Advance Base, only to be driven back because of low temperature, a sixty-mile blizzard, and engine trouble. Communicating their distress to Advance Base, they were ordered by the lonely watcher there to turn back and to take no further risks to reach him.

Anxiety cast a pall over Little America. Only a few words came in by radio, and his companions were convinced that something serious had happened to their leader. But they were helpless to break through the hostile blackness, the omnipresent drifts, and the unabating wind. On August fourth tractor number one, in charge of Thomas Poulter, set out again. On the seventh day of their heroic journey they caught sight of a winking light. Pressing forward, they drew near to the flame of the magnesium flare. At length their searchlight picked up a man in furs walking slowly toward them. "Come on down, fellows," he said, "I have a bowl of hot soup for you." His tractor crew realized something of what he had been through when they saw the litter of cans under the bunk and the final instructions that were hanging from a nail. The meteorological records were complete.

Poulter radioed Little America, "The fumes from the stove got R. E. B. down about June first. Please don't publish as it would be hard on his wife."

"For God's sake," somebody at camp snapped at radio officer Dyer as the word came through, "tell Poulter we want to know how Byrd is."

The answer floated back: "Pretty weak now, but think he will pull through."

Poulter writes of this dramatic meeting: "When we did reach the Advance Base in August we were scarcely two weeks ahead of the sun. His need for aid had passed. He had fought it out alone and wholly within himself in June and, in spite of recurring periods of weakness, he was once more struggling uphill. I don't know of anything finer than that in life or literature. The odds were so overwhelmingly against him that he should rightfully have lost the fight. Had he done so, his chivalrous regard for us would have been only too evident. It is natural that he should have our deep gratitude, for what he endured and for his willingness to face the supreme sacrifice in his thoughtfulness for our safety."

Admiral Byrd's lonely vigil is not only a thrilling proof of human heroism; it is noteworthy because of the spiritual experience that came to the explorer in his solitude. His vision completed the thoughts that came to him as he flew over the North Pole, and was to initiate a new epoch in his life. These words were written in his diary in the hours of his deepest testing:

"I find that I must take charge of my mind or it will take charge of me. One of my diversions is to try to get an unprejudiced mental picture of civilization. The distance and detachment of this place seem to soften some human follies. Others take on added significance. But from here the great folly of all follies is the amazing attitude of civilized nations towards each other. It seems a great madness. If this attitude is not changed, I don't see how our civilization, as we know it, will survive. I wonder if it is possible that the infinite diversions of civilization act as a narcotic to dull the mind of the human race to its danger?

"Fear, antagonism, and reprisals seem to be the rule among nations which, in their conduct toward each other, are, I believe, twenty thousand years behind the individual civilized citizen in his conduct towards his neighbor. In fact, international relations are often highly primitive.

"The well-being of a nation depends upon the well-being of its neighbor nations and fair and friendly trade relations with those nations.

"Therefore, it appears to me that if a citizen desires reasonable prosperity and well-being for his family and his fellow citizens, he should strive for friendly understanding within the family of nations. That seems the loyal and efficient thing to do for his country. I feel this so keenly that if I survive this ordeal I shall devote what is left of my life largely to trying to help further the friendship of my country with other nations of the world."

On his return to the United States he said, "When I left this country for Antarctica, civilization was in the agony of a depression, the inevitable result of that colossal madness—the World War. Two years later I return to a world that is again threatened with war. The great lesson had not been learned. I find a growing mass fear. Nations everywhere have been swept by a nightmare, and in the resulting terror they are arming to the teeth against the day when the nightmare will come true.

"With so many opportunities for our new science to push out the boundaries of the unknown and build a fairer and better life for human beings, we are using our technological knowledge to prepare a cataclysm which will bring to final ruin all we have achieved in the last three hundred years.

"Even aviation, which was a gift that would tie us together as members of the same human race in knowledge, understanding, and friendship, is being perverted to uses that never were dreamed of. The threat of the airplane, which makes possible the extension of warfare to every city and hamlet of the world, is one of the main causes of the present universal nightmare. It is the fear of wings over the world that is helping to drive us deeper and deeper into international insanity.

"What is the use of new inventions and new knowledge if they lead us only to a Dark Age? Surely there must be some way out of this blind alley into which we have driven ourselves.

"I have great faith that individuals of the human race do not of their free, natural will choose this road that is leading to anarchy, for they want freedom and this common desire should be a bond of union among human beings.

"And now, in conclusion, I propose to carry out the promise I made myself during the long night. Here it is. I shall set aside two years of my life some time later on to further explorations, but as soon as I get some months of greatly needed rest, I shall start my work for international amity, though I realize only too well that my part will be an extremely humble one, for my experience lies in far different fields, and I know also that I am only one of hundreds of millions who are as equally concerned as I am with this great problem."

His determination to help solve humanity's greatest problem has been shown in numerous addresses and public statements made since 1936:

"There are millions of people who think that it is impossible to do anything about war and so are lying down on the job. To let the war monster crush civilization without a struggle is a jellyfish attitude. If the nations of the world put forth one quarter as much effort in stopping war as they do in preparing for it with the ever-increasing armaments, war would most certainly be conquered.

"Is it not high time for the great masses of the people of the world, who suffer the disasters of war, to rise up in righteous wrath and demand that nations stop their quarreling?

"Civilized nations are as individualistic and quarrelsome as sixty-two hermits suddenly brought together to live in a village. Quarrels are inevitable among nations until the law of self-preservation forces the development of the international community spirit. Above all, there must be re-established faith in the pledged word of a nation, and there is need for haste, because the world is getting smaller every year and the nations more interdependent.

"We must also stop the mad armament race. Airplanes, which I at first hoped would be instruments of good will, have become flying cannons of destruction, utilized only too often to kill the sick and women and children. It is inevitable that ever-increasing armaments will do one of two things. They will eventually burst into a great world conflict, or there will be a financial collapse that will bring about another depression that will wipe democracy from the face of the earth."

Active in the No-Foreign-War Crusade, the Emergency Peace Campaign, and other anti-war efforts, Admiral Byrd has, during the past three years, summoned audiences throughout this country to awaken and enlist in civilization's most important crusade, the crusade against war. "Let us use our aggressive instinct," he urged, "to end wholesale killings of our fellow men, rather than to bring about more killings." In pointing out the necessity for international economic co-operation he said, "Man finds it comparatively easy to change his environment but has a very difficult time changing his own practices. He can make better mechanical models every year, but the change in the human model is barely perceptible. In short, man, as a group, has got to change his attitude if he does not want his children and their descendants to be enslaved by the situations produced by the machines he has created.

"Let us come honestly face to face with ourselves. Don't let us shut our eyes to the momentous question mark of the twentieth century, which is man himself. Can man, if he continues to concentrate the major part of his genius on material and mechanical things, successfully hope to rule himself through nations of free peoples with representative forms of government? The dictatorship is an admission that free men cannot rule themselves. Would it not be a wise thing to sidetrack some of this genius for a while into the work of bringing to pass an alliance of groups and then of co-ordinating the effort of that coalition? Coalition is the word for democracy."

I was recently in Admiral Byrd's home at the foot of Beacon Hill in Boston, and found the place teeming with preparations for the third Antarctic Expedition. The intrepid explorer has set forth once more, leaving the comforts of home and the happy circle of his wife and four children, to push back the frontiers of the Antarctic. In this search for knowledge we know that he has one consuming purpose, and that is to chart the "moral limitations of the world," for the "really great explorers will be those who find the way to universal reconstruction."

"I Am an Optimist":

EDOUARD BENEŠ

It was in the lobby of an American country club on a summer afternoon that I talked with Dr. Edouard Beneš, Europe's foremost statesman, who is president of a country that temporarily does not exist. In spite of the conquest of Czechoslovakia by the Nazis, the sturdy little diplomat remains unconquered, vital and alert, a champion of democracy. His close-cropped hair and mustache are iron gray, his blue eyes shrewd, his whole being tense with resolution.

"We need to remember today that truth will prevail." He quoted the famous motto of his predecessor, President Tomas Masaryk. "But we need to qualify that statement, 'Truth will prevail' *if* we do our part. We must fight falsehood and evil! Truth will not prevail if we just sit and take our ease. We must fight against evil. We must contend for right.

"You may conquer the outward form of a nation but never its spirit. The independence of my people has not been crushed; it still exists and cannot be stamped out!" Dr. Beneš held a pair of horn spectacles in his left hand, gesturing with his right hand continually, fingers and thumb held together. "The world will not be mismanaged forever. Tyranny tends to destroy itself. History proves that good will is stronger than guns and the spirit mightier than the sword. Material force can destroy material things, but it cannot destroy a spiritual ideal. Tyrants burned the body of Huss, but not his message. You can destroy the bearer of truth, but not the truth itself. Guns seem today to crush the defenders of liberty, but that does not indicate that liberty is destroyed. The ultimate outcome of history is not determined by my success, nor the success of my generation. Enemies may kill me and I may fail, but success belongs ultimately to the right!"

Who is this scholar-statesman, considered by many to be the greatest political mind in Europe? His parents were peasants. He was the youngest of ten children. His boyhood was spent toiling in the fields of a back-country farm far from a railroad. The hard-won earnings of the farm sent the youngest boy to the college in Prague, where he became an ardent patriot and socialist. He helped to support himself by tutoring. He excelled in association football. The star "outside right" broke his leg while playing for the Slavia team of Prague. That broken leg was of momentous importance, because it released him from military duty. Planning to become a school teacher, he entered the University of Prague, and then went abroad for study. At twenty-one he arrived in Paris with only twelve dollars in his pocket. He scrubbed and cared for his attic room, and did his own cooking. There were three years of physical hunger, poverty, and self-denial spent in the quest for knowledge in five European countries. He writes of those days:

"I had gone abroad to study modern languages and prepare myself for a university professorship in this subject. My fondness for political matters, my bent for the study of social problems, and also material considerations, had caused me to turn to journalism, and from that to the study of law, political science, and sociology. I had occupied myself closely with philosophy while still at Prague in my first university year. As a young student, who had been through hardships, who had been distressed by the political and social conditions at home, I was soon impressed by everything I saw in France and in Paris. I was greatly moved by the whole of the French and Parisian revolutionary tradition; I was carried away by the revolutionary and radical phraseology of the French Socialists, syndicalists, and other Left Wing parties; I was absorbed by the study of extremists movements, revolutionary syndicalism, French Socialism and anti-militarism, anarchism, the French and Russian Revolutions with all their offshoots.

"The endeavor to learn as much as I could abroad, and to acquire sufficient knowledge so that I could return home fully prepared for academic and public activity, urged me on to feverish labor, to fathom rapidly the political, social, and cultural problems of France. From there I passed over to England, and subsequently also to Belgium, Italy, and Germany. The preparation of my thesis for a doctor's degree at the Dijon Faculty of Law compelled me at the same time to make a detailed study of the conditions in my own country and in Austria.

"My stay in Paris brought me also among the Russian Revolutionaries who had taken part in the first Russian Revolution of 1905, and my contact with them made a deep impression upon me. In 1906 and 1907 I visited their meetings at Paris, becoming a member of their societies. I began to make a close study of Russia and of Russian literature, both classical and revolutionary.

"The deepest impressions in these matters, however, were those which I formed in Berlin. The military parade, which was arranged in the summer of 1908 and at which I was present, overwhelmed me. The development of industry and railways, of the Prussian military and naval strength, compared with what I had seen in Paris and London in this respect, the mechanization of all public life under the influence of Prussian discipline, the atmosphere of constraint and the prevailing influence and authority of the military, aristocratic, and bureaucratic caste, affected me painfully, because at that time I was unable to arrive at any clear conclusion as to what it was to lead to. I felt instinctively that it must end disastrously, and the effect which it produced upon me . . . was a disturbing one.

"Returning to Prague in 1908, I had two further aims: to see Russia and to secure a living at home by obtaining a teaching post. I also thought of qualifying for a university professorship, spending some time in special academic work. Then, after adequate political preparation and training—I reckoned that I should have to devote at least another ten years to self-education and political preparation—I would make an attempt to enter politics. Accordingly, between 1908 and 1914, I studied political economy, sociology, and philosophy, preparing for my professorship and university duties."

Five years of study, teaching, and writing followed at the university, and then the World War burst upon Europe. Dr. Beneš called on Dr. Masaryk to present a complete plan of a war for liberation that called for passive resistance at home and co-operation with the Allies abroad, and culminated in revolution against the Austro-Hungarian Empire and the creation of a new republic made up of Czechs and Slovaks. Like Masaryk, he was an ardent Czech nationalist who believed in following progressive western nations. His own people must learn from the West, not from the East. They must become realistic, learn to observe and modernize.

The dangerous game of revolution called for daring and nerves of steel. Masaryk went to Switzerland. Beneš remained in Prague to organize Mafia, an underground society that spied on Austria-Hungary, gave information to the Allies, and laid plans for Czech independence. A pipeline of information was kept open through code and newspaper advertisements, foreign literature was smuggled in, and journalists who could write in French and English were smuggled out to help convince the Allies to back the Czech cause.

In the summer of 1915 Beneš was threatened with arrest. He asked his neighbor, a police officer, to try to protect his library; then he went into the country to say good-bye to his wife. He told her he would probably not see her for two years. She must be prepared for hardship; perhaps imprisonment. Should conditions become unbearable, she was to repudiate him. With a forged passport and a little handbag that held all he was permitted to take with him, he took the train for the border. It was four years before he was to see his wife again. She was to suffer imprisonment and undergo loneliness and privation. But, as he said to her on parting, "Every great cause demands sacrifices, and they must be made resolutely, without sentimentality."

With a price on his head, Beneš slipped through the Bavarian frontier and escaped to Switzerland. Joining Masaryk, he became chief of staff. They organized the Czechoslovak National Council in France, England, Russia, and the United States—units that worked for the overthrow of the Hapsburg empire. *The New Europe*, a weekly review published in English, was the chief mouthpiece of their political campaign. They insisted that there could be no peace in Europe so long as the political map was not brought into accord with the natural distribution of the people. The Congresses of Vienna and Berlin had fastened an alien domination on some eighty million people. These two organizers presented their case to the Allied nations and won their support. They created out of Czech exiles and refugees three armies, in Russia, France, and Italy; they brought the Czechs of the world into one crusade for freedom; and, finally, they gained recognition for their country-to-be from the Allied powers.

When war came to an end, the republic of Czechoslovakia was established, with Masaryk as president and Beneš as foreign minister. Through the post-war years, Beneš became one of the constructive leaders of Europe. He was one of the best debaters and thinkers in the League of Nations. Moderation and sincerity were among his virtues. He saw the folly of vindicative nationalism, advocated reconciliation with Germany, and urged peaceful co-operation among all nations.

When Masaryk died, Beneš succeeded his beloved friend as president of the well-established republic. But circumstances conspired against the new president. Adolf Hitler was thundering that the names Versailles and Beneš were one, that the problem was not that of Czechoslovakia but of Beneš. The twentieth anniversary of the republic drew near as thirty divisions of German troops were massed on the borders of the peace-loving nation. Czechoslovakia was deserted by her allies, who urged Beneš to sacrifice himself and his people to keep peace in Europe. Surrender to tyranny was inevitable; there was no alternative.

Beneš bore the humiliation with admirable dignity and fortitude. But when the exile reached London, it was noted that his iron physique and iron nerve had been broken by the terrific strain. After a rest in England, he came to the University of Chicago as lecturer, and has been very active in America, traveling widely to address great audiences and to work with the Czech people. They still speak of him as the president, and technically they are right. It requires an order of the National Assembly at Prague to vote the republic out of being. That action has not been taken.

The National Council in Chicago forms a center of great power, with its affiliated councils in London and Paris. Many of the officers of the army left Czechoslovakia and are organizing in other countries, ready to support their comrades at home. There are thirty thousand Czechs organized in France. There are legations and consulates in many countries that do not recognize the Hitler coup. They form a diplomatic network. In the former republic, citizens hold faithful allegiance to the Party of National Unity and settle down to passive resistance against the government that curbs their liberties and exploits their country. Czech leaders in the United States, rallying about Dr. Beneš, support fifty newspapers, maintain contact with the homeland, aid refugees, unify Czech opinion around the world, hold before the nations the crime that has been committed, and rally public opinion for the restoration of liberty at the center of Europe.

In Prague, someone painted in huge letters on a great rock above the capitol, "We don't want your pfennigs! We want Beneš!" Meanwhile, the president without a country campaigns tirelessly, secure in the affirmation, "I have confidence in the future!"

Dr. Beneš impressed me as a man of discipline—a scholar trained in the search for truth, a diplomat who knew the rigor of seventeen years as foreign secretary and three years as president, a pioneer in democracy and internationalism. This statesman disdains the tricks of the demagogue, makes no cheap concessions to the masses, bases his appeal on fact and not emotion. He defies the dictator and imperialist with the assurance that truth is on his side and that truth is bound to win. As I talked with him I recalled the words of George Lansbury, of England, who said, "Beneš does not understand the word fear and has no room in his mind for hatred."

He holds a rigid discipline over himself. He does not use even the mildest alcoholic drinks and does not smoke. He prefers the simplest of foods. His recreations are walking and tennis. When a student in Paris, he wrote to his brother, "Send me some cheap lithographs. I want them for the bare walls of my room. I cannot stand these French pictures of nakedness." The discipline of fifty-four years has created an invincible will. Happily married, but without children, the Czech patriot dedicates himself completely to his people and the cause of democracy.

"Europe cannot be safe otherwise than as a whole," he stated in the summer of 1939. "To divide one part of Europe from the rest means merely to postpone solutions and to prolong sufferings of one part for the transitory advantage of the other. Such an arrangement could never last.

"In my opinion, the Great War was a clash between the old aristocratic and militarist system and the new liberal and democratic conceptions as they had grown out of the French and American revolutions one and a half centuries ago. The democracies won this conflict, tried to build up a democratic Europe, and even attempted radical solutions of social questions. With idealistic fervor they created a democratic and pacifist international order on the basis of the League of Nations. But a few years after the World War it was already obvious that many European countries were not sufficiently prepared for this change of outlook: there came a reaction in the shape of authoritarian governments and a return to the old national power politics, and what internationalism persisted often veered toward a communist internationalism.

"Times like the present, when all traditions are ruthlessly broken, when there are no firm philosophical, religious, moral, and legal concepts generally accepted—times in which political and social regimes are abolished brutally, without thought of treaties or loyal methods of agreement and when new regimes are created in violent and frequently sanguinary social and political struggles—form a period of upheaval and revolution. These are also times in which the whole life of society is thrown into intellectual chaos, times of moral and intellectual crisis, I do not doubt that this great political and intellectual struggle will come to an end.

"The reaction will come and in the darkest hours it is already on the way. Today in England, in France, even in Germany and Italy, you can watch new spiritual currents, struggles for a new philosophy, a new morality, a new law, and a new political science. . . . A new and better synthesis between the freedom of the individual man on the one side, and of state authority on the other side, will again be realized. Human personality must find a more satisfactory relalation to the community. The nation must find a more satisfactory relation to humanity as a whole and to the international community; the egoisms of nation and state must again recede before international co-operation, and economic self-sufficiency must make room for international trade and economic co-operation.

"The whole historical development of mankind is and always has been one gigantic, heroic struggle for the realization of a constantly higher and juster, a socially and morally more advanced, freedom of the human personality, which by its high moral standard and its fine education would comprehend its duties to the authority of the state, to society as a whole, which could be disciplined and yet have an inner freedom of the spirit, which would show a spontaneous readiness to understand its social and national duties and at the same time not be subjected to any mechanical discipline or authority. I see then which system, dictatorship or democracy, is in my opinion superior. That is why I stand behind democracy and defend it from conviction and shall defend it to the end of my life."

"Will the extreme nationalism of our time destroy itself?" I asked him.

"It is my conviction that it will," he answered. "That seems to me inevitable. It may be the rôle of Hitler and Mussolini to reduce nationalism to an absurdity, and to awaken the world to its dangerous limitations."

"Will we ever evolve a system of international co-operation through which we can restrain war?"

He looked across the room meditatively for a moment, and then answered, "From the beginning of time the great philosophers have taught man how to live. In the simplest of terms they have portrayed the value of human co-operation and peace. History is a great teacher, but, alas, man is such a poor pupil." The look of weariness crept over his face again as if he were conscious of the burden of blundering humanity. "The violence and barbarism of today are due to human stupidity, to the folly of following the lies of false leaders. We speak of the dark ages of the past that marked the low ebb of human reason. It is midnight now in Europe! In spite of the darkness, I am an optimist. I am an optimist because I am a realist."

I thought of Dr. Beneš' reputation as a hard-headed realist who insisted on the facts and enjoyed the reputation of being one of the best informed men in Europe on politics, economics, sociology and philosophy. He had known every type of diplomat from Litvinov to Chamberlain. For twenty years he had been a leading actor in the volcanic drama of European affairs.

"What is the greatest evil in the world today?" I asked again. "Is it fear, prejudice, or economic insecurity?"

"I should answer no one of these evils, but rather moral degeneracy. Our world is blighted by decadence of moral conscience. We are becoming callous to human suffering, to injustice and exploitation. Conscience has been dulled and blighted."

"If you were dictator of the world, what would be your first move?"

His blue eyes flashed. "Well, in the first place I could never be a dictator. If elected, I'd resign. But if I were given a chance to tackle the world's gravest problem, I'd move for moral awakening, for a moral renaissance.

America is not so far advanced in the process of moral decay. You are a younger democracy, and your conditions are healthier. For many reasons America is in a position to exert moral leadership in an immoral world. In spite of the crimes that blight the earth, we must not give up the fight."

As I said good bye to Dr. Beneš I thought of Mayor LaGuardia's words: "I admire Beneš. He is every inch a fighter!" He is a formidable foe of tyranny, a bold challenger of fascism, a gambler who stakes everything on his belief in democracy, the man who may be destined to stop the dictators of Europe.

"I hope you will go back to Prague some day," I said as I turned to go.

"I expect to!" He gripped my hand firmly. "And to live there again with a *free* people!"

---

*"It Is the Struggle that
   Gives Value to Life":*

JAWAHARLAL NEHRU

THE ten-year-old Indian boy longed to grow up to win freedom for his people. He was stirred to the depths as he heard his father, a successful and wealthy lawyer, discuss the conduct of the white man in India. It was a humiliation for his race to be subject to the English. "Instances of conflicts between the rulers and the ruled were common and were fully discussed," he states. "It was a notorious fact that whenever an Englishman killed an Indian he was acquitted by a jury of his own countrymen. In railway trains compartments were reserved for Europeans, and, however crowded the train might be—and they used to be terribly crowded—no Indian was allowed to travel in them, even though they were empty. Even an unreserved compartment would be taken possession of by an Englishman, and he would not allow any Indian to enter it. Benches and chairs were also reserved for Europeans in public parks and other places.

"I was filled with resentment against the alien rulers of my country who misbehaved in this manner, and whenever an Indian hit back I was glad. Not infrequently one of my cousins or one of their friends became personally involved in these individual encounters, and then of course we all got very excited over it. One of the cousins was the strong man of the family and he loved to pick a quarrel with an Englishman, or more frequently with Eurasians, who, perhaps to show off their oneness with the ruling race, were often even more offensive than the English official or merchant. Such quarrels took place especially during railway journeys."

Jawaharlal was an only son. His father was an outstanding lawyer in Allahabad, a progressive and intelligent man. There were a large garden, a swimming pool, and electric lights in their big city home. Ambitious to give the best to his son, his father took him to England in 1905, when he was fifteen, and placed him in Harrow. After three years at Harrow, he went on to Cambridge, where he took his degree in 1910. For two years he studied law in London and passed the Bar examinations. There was plenty of money to spend, and he often exceeded his handsome allowance. He called himself a Cyrenaic, seeking to gratify by means of a Greek name his "desire for a soft life and pleasant experiences. I was superficial and did not go down deep into anything. The aesthetic side of life appealed to me, and the idea of going through life worthily, not indulging in the vulgar way, but still making the most of it and living a full and many-sided life, attracted me. I tried to ape the prosperous but somewhat empty-headed Englishman who is called a 'man about town.' This soft and pointless existence, needless to say, did not improve me in any way. My early enthusiasms began to tone down, and the only thing that seemed to go up was my conceit."

After seven years in England the young lawyer returned to India, a handsome fellow in his tailored western clothes, but something of a dandy and a prig. India was overwhelmingly different: the teeming masses, the low standards of living, the slow tempo of life. He felt bitterly dissatisfied with himself and his environment. He longed to enter politics, but what had politics to offer when he was part of a subject people?

The World War overclouded national activities. "There was little sympathy with the British in spite of loud professions of loyalty," he wrote of this period. "Moderate and extremist alike learnt with satisfaction of German victories. There was no love for Germany, of course, only the desire to see our own rulers humbled. It was the weak and helpless man's idea of vicarious revenge. I suppose most of us viewed the struggle with mixed feelings. Toward all the nations involved, my sympathies were probably most with France. The ceaseless and unabashed propaganda on behalf of the Allies had some effect, although we tried to discount it greatly."

The end of the war found India in a state of suppressed excitement. Industrialism had spread. The capitalist class had grown in power and were eager for more. The middle class demanded constitutional change and a larger measure of self-rule. Soldiers returning from Europe were not willing to continue as subservient slaves. The Rowlatt Bills were passed, with their drastic provisions for arrest and trial without any of the checks and formalities that the law should provide. A wave of anger against England surged over India.

Gandhi appealed to the viceroy not to consent to the Rowlatt Bills; and when his appeal was rejected, he started the *satyagraha* movement of non-violent resistance. He came to talk with Jawaharlal and his father about the program of passive resistance. His father did not want him to risk prison for his convictions. They discussed the problem and were for days in a mental conflict. The son felt that he must follow Gandhi even though it made him turn against his father's will. Night after night he would wander alone, tortured in mind, trying to grope his way out. His father slept on the floor to find out how it would feel to be in prison. *Satyagraha Day* brought all-India demonstrations and complete suspension of business; firing by the police and military at Delhi and Amritsar, and the killing of many people; mob violence in Amritsar and Ahmedabad; the massacre of Jallianwala Bagh; the long horror and terrible indignity of martial law in the Punjab. The Punjab was cut off from the rest of India; a thick veil seemed to cover it and hide it from outside eyes. Jawaharlal sought to get to the Punjab and defy the martial law regulations. He wanted to identify himself with the masses.

Up to this point he had been bourgeois in his politics. He now realized that he was ignorant of labor conditions in factories and on farms. He became interested in the *kisan* (peasant) movement, touched by the tragedy of their lot. "Early in June 1920," he records, "about two hundred *kisans* marched fifty miles from the interior of Partabgarh district to Allahabad city with the intention of drawing the attention of the prominent politicians there to their woebegone condition. They were led by a man named Ramachandra, who himself was not a local peasant. I learnt that these *kisans* were squatting on the river bank, on one of the Jumna *ghats* [landing place], and, accompanied by some friends, went to see them. They told us of the crushing exactions of the taluqdars [local officials], of inhuman treatment, and that their condition had become wholly intolerable. They begged us to accompany them back to make inquiries as well as to protect them from the vengeance of the taluqdars, who were angry at their having come to Allahabad on this mission. They would accept no denial, and literally clung to us. At last I promised to visit them two days or so later."

He found the peasant crowds in miserable rags, their faces full of excitement. "They showered their affection on us and looked on us with loving and hopeful eyes, as if we were the bearers of good tidings, the guides who were to lead them to the promised land. Looking at them and their misery and overflowing gratitude, I was filled with shame and sorrow: shame at my own easy-going and comfortable life and our petty politics of the city, which ignored this vast multitude of semi-naked sons and daughters of India; sorrow at the degradation and overwhelming poverty of India. A new picture of India seemed to rise before me—naked, starving, crushed, and utterly miserable. And their faith in us, casual visitors from the distant city, embarrassed me and filled me with a new responsibility that frightened me.

"I listened to their innumerable tales of sorrow, their crushing and ever-growing burden of rent, illegal exactions, ejectments from land and mud hut, beatings; surrounded on all sides by vultures who preyed on them—zamindar's [landlord's] agents, money-lenders, police; toiling all day to find that what they produced was not theirs and that their reward was kicks and curses and a hungry stomach. The land was rich, but the burden on it was very heavy, the holdings were small, and there were too many people after them. Taking advantage of this land hunger, the landlords, unable under the law to enhance their rents beyond a certain percentage, charged huge illegal premiums. The tenant, knowing of no other alternative, borrowed money from the money-lender and paid the premium, and then, unable to pay his debt or even the rent, was ejected and lost all he had.

"I spent three days in the villages, came back to Allahabad, and then went again. During these brief visits we wandered about a great deal from village to village, eating with the peasants, living with them in their mud huts, talking to them for long hours, and often addressing meetings, big and small.

"It was the hottest time of year, June, just before the monsoon. The sun scorched and blinded. I was quite unused to going out in the sun, and ever since my return from England I had gone to the hills for part of every summer. And now I was wandering about all day in the open sun with not even a sun-hat, my head wrapped in a small towel. So full was I of other matters that I quite forgot about the heat, and it was only on my return to Allahabad, when I noticed the rich tan I had developed, that I remembered what I had gone through. I was pleased with myself, for I realized that I could stand the heat with the best of them and my fear of it was wholly unjustified. I have found that I can bear both extreme heat and great cold without much discomfort, and this has stood me in good stead in my work as well as in my periods in prison."

Once identified with the masses, he was lifted up by new enthusiasm, and was possessed by the happiness of one who was crusading for a cause. He gave himself wholeheartedly to *satyagraha*, which he believed was the best way to cope with India's oppressors and to arouse the populace to the need for a new state.

Gandhi's famous appeal on *The Doctrine of the Sword* impressed the young lawyer: "I am not a visionary. I claim to be a practical idealist. The religion of non-violence is not meant merely for the *Rishis* [sages] and saints. It is meant for the common people as well. Non-violence is the law of our species as violence is the law of the brute. The spirit lies dormant in the brute and he knows no law but that of physical might. The dignity of man requires obedience to a higher law—to the strength of the spirit.

"I have therefore ventured to place before India the ancient law of self-sacrifice. For *satyagrah* and its off-shoots, non-co-operation and civil resistance, are nothing but new names for the law of suffering. The *Rishis,* who discovered the law of non-violence in the midst of violence, were greater geniuses than Newton. They were themselves greater warriors than Wellington. Having themselves known the use of arms, they realized their uselessness and taught a weary world that its salvation lay not through violence but through non-violence.

"Non-violence in its dynamic condition means conscious suffering. It does not mean meek submission to the will of the evil-doer, but it means the putting of one's whole soul against the will of the tyrant. Working under this law of our being, it is possible for a single individual to defy the whole might of an unjust empire to save his honor, his religion, his soul; and lay the foundation for that empire's fall or regeneration.

"And so I am not pleading for India to practise non-violence because it is weak. I want her to practise non-violence being conscious of her strength and power. . . . I want India to recognize that she has a soul that cannot perish, and that can rise triumphant above any physical weakness and defy the physical combination of a whole world. . . ."

Nehru said, "What I admired was the moral and ethical side of our movement and of *satyagraha*. I did not give an absolute allegiance to the doctrine of non-violence or accept it forever, but it attracted me more and more, and the belief grew upon me that, situated as we were in India and with our background and traditions, it was the right policy for us. The spiritualization of politics, using the word not in its narrow religious sense, seemed to me a fine idea."

Because they were active in the boycott of foreign cloth, he and his father were arrested. During December, 1921, and January, 1922, some thirty thousand persons were sentenced to imprisonment in connection with the non-co-operation movement. During the next thirteen years the number of political offenders sent to prison was to reach the total of three hundred thousand men and women.

The superintendent of the Lucknow jail did not like to see young Nehru reading so much in his cell. He considered it a dangerous pastime. He admitted that he had finished his general reading at the age of twelve. No doubt, his prisoner surmised, this abstention had been of use to the English colonel in avoiding troublesome thoughts and helped him to rise to the position of Inspector-General of Prisons in the United Provinces.

"One misses many things in prison," the famous prisoner wrote, "but perhaps most of all one misses the sound of women's and children's laughter. The sounds one usually hears are not of the pleasantest. The voices are harsh and minatory, and the language brutal and largely consisting of swear-words. Once I remember being struck by a new want. I was in the Lucknow District Gaol, and I realized suddenly that I had not heard a dog bark for seven or eight months."

After his release he was elected to the headship of the Allahabad municipality, and was forced to cope with the problems of an Indian city. So much time was now given to municipal work and to Congress that he withdrew from his law practice. Advantageous offers came from large industrial firms, but he turned them down, because he was determined to work for the good of India. It made him feel uncomfortable to depend on his father financially, but his father had sufficient income to care for his son's family, and was glad to do it. Their style of living had undergone considerable change since 1920. Horses and carriages had been sold, superfluous furniture disposed of, and the number of servants reduced. There was still enough for essentials, but the whole house was reorganized on the basis of simplicity. Jawaharlal wore *khadi* (homespun) clothes and traveled third class on the railways.

Unrest among the Sikhs in the Nabla state led the British administrator to prohibit participation in an annual religious ceremony. As a protest, groups of Sikhs were sent to the temple at Jaito. The delegations were stopped, beaten by the police, arrested, and usually carried to an out-of-the-way place in the jungle and left there. Nehru had read of these beatings and went to investigate. As a result he was thrown into prison, where he contracted typhoid fever. Soon after, his wife became seriously ill, and they went to Switzerland in search of health.

On his return he became secretary of the Congress and plunged again into political activities. During a demonstration against the Simon Commission, which was then in India, the popular leader Lala Lajpat Rai was beaten with a police club by a young English officer. He died as a result, and the masses were stirred to resentment. Nehru took part in a protest procession in Lucknow and was beaten by a mounted policeman with his long stick. The city was aroused, and the next day a great demonstration was staged at the time the Simon Commission arrived.

"There was a huge open space, about half a mile square, in front of the station, and we were made to line up on one side of this *maidan* and there our procession remained, making no attempt to push our way forward. The place was full of foot and mounted police, as well as the military. The crowd of sympathetic onlookers swelled up, and many of these persons managed to spread out in twos and threes in the open space. Suddenly we saw in the far distance a moving mass. They were two or three long lines of cavalry or mounted police covering the entire area, galloping down towards us, and striking and riding down the numerous stragglers that dotted the *maidan*. Behind the charging lines people lay on the ground, some still unable to move, others writhing in pain, and the whole appearance of that *maidan* was that of a battlefield. But we did not have much time for gazing on that scene or for reflections; the horsemen were soon upon us, and their front line clashed almost at a gallop with the massed ranks of our processionists. We held our ground, and, as we appeared to be unyielding, the horses had to pull up at the last moment, reared up on their hind legs with their front hoofs quivering in the air over our heads. And then began a beating of us, and battering with *lathis* [bamboo rods] and long batons both by the mounted and the foot police. It was a tremendous hammering, and the clearness of vision that I had had the evening before left me. All I knew was that I had to stay where I was, and must not yield or go back."

Some of Nehru's admirers carried him from the front line, believing that the police were determined to kill him.

"Now that the excitement of the moment had passed," he wrote later, "I felt pains all over my body and great fatigue. Almost every part of me seemed to ache, and I was covered with contused wounds and marks of blows. But fortunately I was not injured in any vital spot.

"But the memory that endures with me, far more than that of the beating itself, is that of many of the faces of those policemen, and especially of the officers, who were attacking us. Most of the real beating and battering was done by European sergeants, the Indian rank and file being milder in their methods. And those faces, full of hate and blood-lust, almost mad, with no trace of sympathy or touch of humanity!

"The excitement of action held us; but, as it passed immediately the question arose: To what end was all this? To what end?"

In 1929 Gandhi made his *khad* tour of the United Provinces, and Nehru accompanied him. It was the hottest season of the year and exhausting work. Human beings swarmed together like locusts to hear their great prophet. As they motored across the country they would stop every few miles to greet multitudes of ten to twenty-five thousands, while the principal meeting of the day would exceed one hundred thousand. Nehru marvelled at the powers of Gandhi, his endurance, his ability, his popularity, but he did not agree with him completely.

"In those days Gandhi was collecting funds for *khadi* work, and he would say frequently that he wanted money for the Lord of the poor, or God who resides in the poor; meaning thereby that he wanted it to help the poor to find employment and work in cottage industries. But behind that word there seemed to be a glorification of poverty; God was especially the Lord of the poor; they were his chosen people. That, I suppose, is the usual religious attitude everywhere. I could not appreciate it, for poverty seemed to me a hateful thing, to be fought and rooted out and not to be encouraged in any way. This inevitably led to an attack on a system which tolerated and produced poverty, and those who shrank from this had of necessity to justify poverty in some way. They could only think in terms of security and could not picture a world abundantly supplied with the necessaries of life; probably, according to them, the rich and the poor would always be with us."

The younger man believed that Gandhi did not go far enough. In 1929, Gandhi, refusing to serve as president of the All-India Congress, pressed the names of Nehru, who was elected to this position of high influence. That winter a festival was held in Allahabad, and throngs of pilgrims came each day to his home. He spoke to them, listened to their troubles, and received the tokens of their admiration. He realized that he was popular with the masses as well as with the intelligentsia, and a hero of Indian youth. Songs were written about him; legends began to spring up. A rich lawyer was sacrificing everything for India. His renunciation made a dramatic appeal.

Nehru himself did not like this view of renunciation. He said, "I prefer the active virtues to passive ones, and renunciation and sacrifice for their own sakes have little appeal for me. I do value them from another point of view—that of mental and spiritual training—just as a simple and regular life is necessary for the athlete to keep in good physical condition. And the capacity for endurance and perseverance in spite of hard knocks is essential for those who wish to dabble in great undertakings. But I have no liking or attraction for the ascetic view of life, the negation of life, the terrified abstention from its joys and sensations. I have not consciously renounced anything that I really valued; but then values change.

"My real conflict lay within me, a conflict of ideas, desires and loyalties, of subconscious depths struggling with outer circumstances, of an inner hunger unsatisfied. I became a battle ground where various forces struggled for mastery. I sought an escape from this; I tried to find harmony and equilibrium, and in this attempt I rushed into action. That gave me some peace; outer conflict relieved the strain of the inner struggle."

In 1930, Gandhi urged the people to resist the salt tax, and civil disobedience was organized. Gandhi was arrested; and Nehru was sent back to Naini prison in solitary confinement. There was a little circular enclosure in which he slept outdoors on hot nights, from which he would study the stars. He found it comforting to watch the constellations. But he was restless, as this record shows:

"The thought that I was having a relatively easy time in prison, at a time when others were facing danger and suffering outside, began to oppress me. I longed to go out, and, as I could not do that, I made my life in prison a hard one, full of work. I used to spin daily for nearly three hours on my own *charkha* [spinning wheel]; for another two or three hours I did weaving, which I had especially asked for from the jail authorities. I liked these activities. They kept me occupied without undue strain or requiring too much attention, and they soothed the fever of my mind. I read a great deal, and otherwise busied myself with cleaning up, washing my clothes, and other forms of manual labor."

The main purpose of prison was not to improve and help the unhappy individuals who came to it. Break them! That was the idea; so that by the time they went out they would not have the least bit of spirit left in them. After his release he was allowed eight days of freedom; and then was rearrested on the charge of sedition and agitation against the salt tax. It was his fifth term; the sentence was for two years and five months. He was later discharged because of his father's illness; and was with him when he died. He himself broke down in health and went to Ceylon for a change. Everywhere people crowded to see him, and he was in continual demand as a speaker. Returning to India, he engaged in study of the peasant and his problems. The peasants were the victims of money lenders, who took their property from them and became proprietors on a large scale. In the Allahabad district, thousands of peasants had been dispossessed. They besieged Nehru's home, begging for relief. He was convinced that a land system which permitted such indebtedness, poverty, and despair must be changed.

"The land problem," he pointed out, "is the outstanding problem in India; and any final solution of it is difficult to see without revolutionary changes in our agriculture and land system. Feudal relics and the big landlord system are hindrances to development and will have to go. The tiny holdings, averaging a fraction of an acre per person, are uneconomic and wasteful and too small for the application of scientific methods. Large-scale state and collective or co-operative farms must be established, and this cannot be done so long as the vested interests in land are not removed."

Better farms, better homes, better schools, better sanitation; these must come or the masses of India will rise in revolution. The static period is over, he points out. A hunger for change and for the ending of misery and poverty has seized the masses.

From 1933 through 1935 the crusader was again in prison, where he wrote an autobiography that forms one of the most stirring contemporary documents. He gave certain hours each day to writing, to manual work, and to physical exercise. His favorite exercise was "standing on my head with the palms of my hands, fingers interlocked, supporting the back of my head, elbows on the floor, body vertical, upside down. I suppose physically this exercise is very good; I liked it even more for its psychological effect on me. The slightly comic position increased my good humor and made me a little more tolerant of life's vagaries."

The handsome, impetuous social prophet outlines his views on the independence of India in this fashion. For years he has been battling for the self-government of his people. It is natural and inevitable that they should stand on their own feet. For many generations the British treated India as an enormous country house. They were the gentry owning the house and occupying the desirable parts of it, while the Indians were consigned to the servants' hall and pantry and kitchen. A fixed hierarchy was established, an impassable barrier between classes. Sometimes, if the servants were good, they were allowed to go to the drawing room for a cup of tea. But all this has changed. The servants no longer feel pride in their gold braid. They do not intend to go on forever taking orders from a little group of white men who exploit them. Many times in prison he has suffered anxiety and discomfort, but he says that he has never hated an English brother. He does, however, dislike British imperialism and resent its imposition upon India. He demands that the exploitation of India shall cease, among all who exploit, whether they be white or brown; and that a new state and a new government shall be established for the common man, who makes up the millions of India.

Nehru is more aggressive than Gandhi, more modern, more intent on social and economic revolution. With his high admiration for the *Mahatma,* he believes that he is too much of a medieval saint who does not fit with contemporary needs. He questions the value of the ascetic life. There has been too much self-mortification in the Orient, too much self-negation. Human beings must be awakened to the divine possibilities of life in the present world. He disagrees with Gandhi's ideas on sex and marriage and advocates normal, wholesome relationships between husband and wife. He denies that there is any virtue in poverty, and demands that the poor must be redeemed and uplifted. He questions the value of non-resistance in dealing with western nations. India must resist with more vigor than she has shown before.

He thinks it folly to recover the primitive economic practices of a pre-industrial age. India must welcome the industrial age. She must modernize. "Present-day civilization is full of evils, but it is also full of good; and it has the capacity in it to rid itself of those evils. To destroy it root and branch is to remove that capacity from it and revert to a dull, sunless, and miserable existence. But even if that were desirable it is an impossible undertaking. We cannot stop the river of change or cut ourselves adrift from it and psychologically we who have eaten of the apple of Eden cannot forget that taste and go back to primitiveness."

Nehru is outspoken on religion. He tells Hindu and Moslem that they cannot hope to remain separate and apart from other faiths and other cultures in an age when swift travel, world news, radio, and cinema bind all men and morals together. No philosophy can resist modern scientific, industrial civilization. "India is supposed to be a religious country above everything else," he says, "and Hindu, Moslem, Sikh, and others take pride in their faiths and testify to their truth by breaking heads. The spectacle of what is called religion, or at any rate organized religion, in India and elsewhere has filled me with horror, and I have frequently condemned it and wished to make a clean sweep of it. Almost always it seems to stand for blind belief and reaction, dogma and bigotry, superstition and exploitation. And the preservation of vested interests. And yet I knew well that there was something else in it, something which supplied a deep inner craving of human beings. How else could it have been the tremendous power it has been, and brought peace and comfort to innumerable tortured souls? Was that peace merely the shelter of blind belief and absence of questioning, the calm that comes from being safe in harbor, protected from the storms of the open sea, or was it something more? In some cases certainly it was something more."

Religion, he insists, must seek truth no matter what the sacrifice, and must share life with humanity. He traces his vision of a better world in these words: "Our final aim can only be a classless society with equal economic justice and opportunity for all, a society organized on a planned basis for the raising of mankind to higher material and cultural levels, to a cultivation of spiritual values, of co-operation, unselfishness, the spirit of service, the desire to do right, good will, and love—ultimately a world order. Everything that comes in the way will have to be removed, gently if possible, forcibly if necessary."

In 1937 Gandhi chose Nehru as his successor as the president of the All-India Congress. The elections proved the organizing power of this gifted leader. In less than a fortnight he covered five thousand miles in a whirlwind campaign, traveling by elephant, camel, car, boat, and plane, to carry his message to the remotest villages. Thirty-three million people went to the polls in this spectacular election. Two years later, the leftist leader, Bose, was elected president. Gandhi, unwilling to follow Bose's radical policies, withdrew his support. Nehru was faced with a difficult decision. He sympathized with many points in the radical program, but he could not desert the *Mahatma*.

It is difficult to prophesy what Nehru's influence will be after the passing of Gandhi. It seems probable that he will become the accepted leader of the masses and one of the great figures of the contemporary world. Meanwhile, he continues his crusade undaunted after lonely vigils in prison cells, years of battling against impregnable resistance, and the long journey under the tormenting burden of starving millions. "The distant mountains seem easy of access and climbing, the top beckons, but, as one approaches, difficulties appear, and the higher one goes the more laborious becomes the journey and the summit recedes into the clouds. Yet the climbing is worth the effort and has its own joy and satisfaction. Perhaps it is the struggle that gives value to life. . . ."

"The Way of Liberty":

LOUIS DEMBITZ BRANDEIS

BECAUSE of their desire for justice and freedom, Adolf and Frederika Brandeis left Bohemia in 1848. Settling in Louisville, Kentucky, they prospered, became the parents of four children and the founders of a cultivated home. Living on the Ohio River, they were conscious of the evils of slavery and tried to help the exploited people about them. Their son, Louis Dembitz, born in 1856, recalls, as one of his earliest memories, going with his mother to carry food to the Civil War soldiers camped near their home.

At the age of fourteen Louis received a diploma from the Louisville High School and a gold medal for "pre-eminence in all studies." Two years later his father's business slumped and the family went to Austria for a long visit. Louis was sent alone to the *Annen-Realschule* in Dresden. He looked over the formidable stone structure with misgivings. Entering reluctantly, he faced the rector's demand for a birth certificate and vaccination certificate with the shrewd argument, "The fact that I am here is proof of my birth and you may look at my arm for evidence that I was vaccinated."

During his second year he returned to the dormitory late one evening, and discovered that he had forgotten his key. Standing under the window of his room, he whistled until his roommate shuffled downstairs to let him in. Someone else heard the whistling. The next morning he was severely reprimanded by the school authorities. The young liberal surged with rebellion. "Back in Kentucky you can whistle," he reasoned. "I'll go back to America. And I'll study to be a lawyer. That's what I've always wanted to be, a lawyer like my uncle, the abolitionist. Nothing else is worth while."

He went back to America to enrol in the Harvard Law School. He was only eighteen, he lacked the usual preparatory courses, and he was forced to earn much of his own expenses. He borrowed two hundred dollars from his brother, started a tutoring business among the college students, and limited his wants to the barest minimum. He gave up smoking because it cut down his efficiency; and stopped playing the violin because he felt he could use his time to better advantage. At the end of his law course, after his brother had been repaid, he had a capital of fifteen hundred dollars. He broke the school record and stood at the head of his class. His classmates elected him as commencement orator. President Eliot called him to his office, "I don't see how you can be the orator. The rule is that the orator is to be a recipient of a degree. You cannot have a degree until you are twenty-one, and you will not be twenty-one until November." Although he was deprived of the honor of making his speech, the young lawyer received his degree.

Five years later he opened the first modern office in Boston, Warren and Brandeis, equipped with a telephone and a stenographer. At the end of the first year the partners had earned a net profit of twelve hundred dollars each. They congratulated each other and went for a horseback ride.

In his thirty-fifth year he married Alice Goldmark. He was already worth fifty thousand dollars. They agreed on a design for living, stoic in simplicity, with an independence from work and worry that would enable him to devote himself to certain "luxuries," such as the defense of the forgotten man, who might be a laborer, policyholder, or consumer. Mrs. Brandeis agreed that he would be happiest by dedicating his leisure and his money to the public good. The heritage of liberty was in his blood.

In 1892 there was a strike in the Carnegie Steel Works

at Homestead, Pennsylvania. Ten strikers were killed and sixty wounded. With the aid of three hundred Pinkerton detectives and eight thousand state militia the company won the strike. "I think it was the affair at Homestead," Brandeis said later, "which first set me thinking seriously about the labor problem. It took the shock of battle, where organized capital hired a private army to shoot at organized labor for resisting an arbitrary cut in wages, to turn my mind definitely toward a searching study of the relations of labor to industry."

He won the title of the "people's attorney" because of his defense of public rights. "The trust problem can never be settled right for the American people," he reasoned, "by looking at it through the spectacles of bonds and stocks. You must study it through the spectacles of people's rights and people's interests; must consider the effect upon the development of the American democracy. When you do that, you will realize the extraordinary perils to our institutions which attend the trust; you will realize the danger of letting the people learn that our sacred Constitution protects not only vested rights but vested wrongs."

Speaking before a Congressional committee about the twelve-hour day, seven-day week, and eighteen-cents-an-hour wage in the steel mills, he picked up a Washington newspaper and read the news that Elbert H. Gary, head of the steel corporation, was intending to give his wife a half-million-dollar string of pearls for Christmas. "Here is what would seem to me a perfect sham of profit-sharing which has been paraded a great deal over this country. See what that means to the social unrest. Isn't it the same sort of thing that brought on the French Revolution, and which may suggest to everyone in this particular connection the damage which the queen's necklace did in those days? That seems to me to be one of the horrible manifestations, the by-products, of this aggregation of capital . . . unearned wealth, unearned by those who are enjoying it, and taken out of the lives of the people who are toiling for them."

In one of his labor cases he appeared before the United States Supreme Court in defense of Oregon's eight-hour law for women. He surprised the court by adding to his brief legal argument a new kind of evidence, nearly one hundred pages, consisting of reports of committees, bureaus of statistics, and commissioners of hygiene. The majority of women in Oregon had been receiving such poor wages that they had been forced to scrimp on food, room in unwholesome quarters, and so sacrifice their health. Many had turned to prostitution to supply themselves with necessities. These conditions, Mr. Brandeis pointed out, were detrimental to the interests of the state. His evidence won the case.

Mrs. Alice N. Lincoln, of Boston, enlisted his help in fighting for reform of the pauper institutions of that city. The buildings on the islands in the harbor were in a tragic state. Drunkards, criminals, paupers, and mental defectives were herded together. After three years of agitation the board of aldermen called a hearing. Mrs. Lincoln gave her testimony, with Brandeis as her counsel. He helped carry her through fifty-seven public headings, proving the wasteful economy of the institutions and their success in turning paupers into criminals. The fees received for this work were all given to charity.

While president of the Aldermanic Association he condemned the corruption of Boston officials, exposing graft and demanding honesty. This was the period when Lincoln Steffens was writing "The Shame of the Cities" for *McClure's Magazine*. Brandeis said, "We cannot submit to the dishonor of being represented by these men. We should not allow ourselves to be represented by thieves and convicts. It is needed that good, honest, honorable men be drafted into service as office holders."

From the beginning of his career Mr. Brandeis has insisted that the legal profession should be more than a business. Lawyers should be free men, and not the tools of corporations. The lawyer should exercise moral courage and take a stand for right and justice, even though it should mean ill will and loss of money. The true exponent of the law should avoid the excesses of vested interests and of the masses.

When I visited the Justice in his Washington apartment in the spring of 1939, he expressed this same conviction to me. He was still the people's attorney, and the defender of liberty through law. It was difficult for me to convince myself that he was in his eighty-third year as I sat in his square, simply furnished study. The shelves of the book case held a few books and stacks of record folders neatly packed into place. The house impressed me with its plainness. The justice sat in a rotary chair, with his back to the desk, which held nothing but a copy of Stefan Zweig's *Erasmus*.

Mr. Brandeis wore a dark gray suit, white shirt, and stiff collar and black tie. His bushy hair was snow white except for a few lingering touches of black. Luminous blue eyes looked out from a face that was marked with the lines of the years, a face that was strong with philosophic serenity. He began with reminiscences of Massachusetts during his early years as a social reformer: his visits to the mill towns throughout the state, his impression of mill owners and workers. They were a good and sturdy people in New England, he observed, and usually reasonable when it came to human betterment. He then turned to his old hobby, savings bank life insurance. "Have you heard much about it in Massachusetts? Do you carry any of it yourself?"

He reminded me that life insurance was not so safe forty years ago as it is today. There was waste and corruption. Companies were not managed for the benefit of the policy holders, but for the benefit of financial interests. Serving as counsel for a group of policy holders he brought to light some of the company practices. The result was a general reorganization of insurance companies, which brought greater security and advantage to the policy holder. Savings bank insurance in Massachusetts was his idea, insurance for the laboring man that was safe and economical. "It took a lot of crusading," he smiled over the memory of those battles. "The companies opposed it, people said it couldn't be done, but we won out. The plan has worked and grown every year."

I thought, as he talked to me, of the plan he is reported to have suggested in 1912. He himself was receiving an income of one hundred thousand dollars a year, and was worth a million and a half dollars. But he was concerned over the problem of unemployment in industry. Too many jobs were insecure, too many men out of work. His plan was to make a deposit in a trust company of a certain part of each week's wages. The average number of days of employment would be calculated at the end of the year, an accounting would be made of the amount of employment exceeding the average, with a division between employer and employee of the amount accumulated. For each day's employment in excess of the standard the employer would take back a part of the deposit; for each day he failed to give employment the worker would receive a part of the fund. A reserve would thus be built up to relieve the worker from the evil of temporary unemployment, and the employer would have an incentive to make improvements to maintain uniformity of employment.

The Justice had lived to see many of his visions come true. As he talked with me I was conscious of his rich background and his clear grasp on the process of social evolution. He quoted date after date as he traced the story of his long study of insurance.

In 1916 President Woodrow Wilson proposed Louis Brandeis' name for the Supreme Court of the United States. Certain financial interests objected strenuously to the appointment. The *New York Press* spoke of him as "a man of furious partisanship, of violent antagonisms, and of irredeemable prejudices." The candidate preserved a philosophic calm in the storm of controversy, reasoning that his record was his defense.

The Senate Judiciary committee made an investigation and approved his appointment. Senator Thomas J. Walsh said of this committee: "The real crime of which this man is guilty is that he has exposed the iniquities of men in high places in our financial system. He has not stood in awe of the majesty of wealth. He has written about and expressed views on 'social justice' . . . movements and measures to attain greater security, greater comfort, and better health for the industrial workers. . . . They all contemplate that a man's a man and not a machine."

President Wilson said of the new Justice, "He is a friend of all just men and a lover of the right; and he knows more than how to talk about the right—he knows how to set it forward in the face of its enemies."

Mrs. Brandeis repaired the old green flannel bag for her husband to use in carrying his papers to the court conferences. And they moved to an apartment in Washington.

This same year he gave an address on "The Living Law" before the Chicago Bar Association. He spoke of the failure of the court to sustain the minimum wage legislation. The trouble was that the law was not living. It had failed to keep pace with the developments in economic, social, and political life. Legal justice had failed to conform with conceptions of social justice. Legal science was tempted to ignore new social needs. The new justice carried his crusade for progress into the court. He was a liberal, who sought "liberty through law."

Louis Brandeis has always had a distrust of bigness. "There used to be a certain glamor about big things," he said. "Anything big, simply because it was big, seemed to be good and great. We are now coming to see that big things may be very bad and mean." Years ago he testified before a Senate Committee on Interstate Commerce, when a study was being made of big business. He raised this warning, "when you increase your business to a very great extent, and the multitude of problems increase with its growth, you will find, in the first place, that the man at the head has a diminishing knowledge of the facts, and, in the second place, a diminishing opportunity for exercising a careful judgment upon them." He challenged the conviction that centralization meant efficiency, and argued that the country's creative powers were being wasted because management was falling into too few hands and a few men were taking on jobs too big for them.

Dissenting in the chain-store case in 1933, he wrote, "There is a wide-spread belief that the existing unemployment is the result, in large part, of the gross inequality in the distribution of wealth and income which giant corporations have fostered . . . that the true prosperity of our past came not from big business, but through the courage, the energy, and the resourcefulness of small men."

"People before things," he insists. "The wealth of a nation lies in the extent to which the creative powers of its people are allowed to function. Every citizen should have a chance to grow to full capacity, in skill, in self-reliance, in leadership.

"Success in any democratic undertaking must proceed from the individual. It is possible only where the process of perfecting the individual is pursued. His development is attained mainly in the process of common living." The full dinner pail is not enough for the citizen. The eight-hour day in most occupations is not too short. Citizens must be in proper physical and mental condition to grope with the problems of modern civilization. It is not enough to enable a peasant to become an agriculturalist; he must also be given the opportunity to become a cultured individual.

"Democracy demands continuous sacrifice by the individual and more exigent obedience to the moral law than any other form of government.

"The great America for which we long is unattainable unless that individuality of communities becomes far more developed. For a century our growth has come through natural expansion and the increase of the functions of the federal government. The growth of the future must be in quality and spiritual value. And that can come only through the concentrated, intensified strivings of smaller groups. The field for special effort should now be the state, the city, the village—and each should be led to seek to excel in something peculiar to it. If ideals are developed locally, the national ones will come pretty near taking care of themselves.

"The makers of the Constitution undertook to secure conditions favorable to the pursuit of happiness. They recognized the significance of man's spiritual nature, of his feelings, and of his intellect. They knew that only a part of the pain, pleasure, and satisfactions in life are to be found in material things. They sought to protect Americans in their beliefs, their thoughts, their emotions and their sensations. They conferred, as against the government, the right to be let alone—the most comprehensive of rights and the right most valued by civilized men."

Under the spell of Mr. Brandeis' personality in the sunny

California Street study that afternoon I was compelled to take seriously some of the legends that circle around this distinguished servant of the law. I admired the independence that he showed when he carried the battered goose-neck desk lamp from the old Supreme Court to the palatial quarters of the new building. He lived simply, not as a miser, but in order that he might keep his mind on more important matters and use his wealth for public good. Concentration on the human equation in life has been the key to his achievement, and has led him to give a fortune to projects of human betterment.

Having heard the report that the Justice started work at five o'clock in the morning, one of his secretaries resolved to find out the truth of the story. He returned to the office after a New Year's Eve party. He waited to see what might happen, somewhat self-conscious in his evening clothes. At five there came the rattle of a key in the lock and the Justice entered. He nodded his customary greeting and sat down quietly to the papers on his desk.

Following the tradition of Thomas Jefferson and Robert E. Lee, Mr. Brandeis turned in the late years of his life to the fathering of a university. His choice was the school of his boyhood home, the University of Louisville. He gave thought, leadership, and money to make the university a seat "not only of learning but of adventure in all fields of intellectual and spiritual endeavor."

As the Justice said good bye, he took a little book from the top of a letter file. "You will find some of my ideas here on the international situation—a Fourth of July oration given in Boston in 1915, but I think the ideas still hold."

The words are pertinent: "America, dedicated to liberty and the brotherhood of man, rejected the aristocratic principle of the superman as applied to peoples as it rejected the principle when applied to individuals. America has believed that each race had something of peculiar value which it can contribute to the attainment of those high ideals for which it is striving. America has believed that we must not only give to the immigrant the best that we have, but must preserve for America the good that is in the immigrant and develop in him the best of which he is capable. America has believed that in differentiation, not in uniformity, lies the path to progress. It acted on this belief; it has advanced human happiness, and it has prospered.

"The movements of the last century have proved that whole peoples have individuality no less marked than that of the single person; that the individuality of a people is irrepressible, and that the misnamed 'internationalism' which seeks the obliteration of nationalities or peoples is unattainable. The new nationalism adopted by America proclaims that each race or people, like each individual, has the right and duty to develop, and that only through such differentiated development will high civilization be attained. Not until these principles of nationalism, like those of democracy, are generally accepted will liberty be fully attained and minorities be secure in their rights. Not until then can the foundation be laid for a lasting peace among the nations."

I lingered for one more question, "As you look back on life, do you think we have made progress?"

"Yes. I think we have made progress. In many ways we are more humane, more concerned with the underprivileged and the exploited, more socially minded. But there are areas of prejudice that are yet to be conquered—the national and racial bitterness that affect our world. This prejudice is a menace to human advance."

"Do you still believe in democracy?"

"Of course. There is no other alternative, is there?"

"You still have faith in the common man?"
"Indeed I do."
"And the future?"
"Yes. I can still look forward!"

Cotton Picker, LL.D.:

MARY McLEOD BETHUNE

She was one of seventeen children. Her parents had been slaves. She had spent a childhood of poverty on the little South Carolina farm weeding and picking cotton. Mary McLeod was the fastest cotton picker on the place. As she dragged the cotton bag up and down the rows she dreamed of the great things that she was to do for herself and her people.

"I wanted to break away," she said, "to shake off imprisoning circumstances and dispel the darkness. I walked six miles through the woods to Sunday school to a humble church with its poorly trained but earnest leaders. How well I remember the revival meetings and the moonlight walks home alone with my soul. I heard God speak, calling me to lead my people.

"Then a little school was opened about five miles away. The worker came to my home and persuaded my parents to let me go. I walked ten miles every day. I was ten or eleven when I went to school for the first time. It was glorious when I felt myself awakening. The fetters were going; life was unfolding. I think my life work must have begun the day I was given a Bible and I was able to read it. That evening mama, papa, and all the family gathered around the fireplace of the tiny cabin, while in faltering words I read from the great book. At that moment I felt the joy of giving something to others."

Destiny led the Negro girl from the little school in Mayesville to Scotia Seminary. A dressmaker in Denver offered to educate a student from the school "if there is one that gives promise of making good." Mary McLeod was chosen for the momentous journey of two hundred and fifty miles to the seminary. Her father made her a wooden trunk, her mother cut down a few old garments, and the neighbors brought in their gifts. They came in by muleback and wagon to see her off on the train journey that led her into a mysterious new world.

Eleven years of study and she began her work as a teacher. She married, took care of her family, and taught school. In the fall of 1904 she determined to start a school of her own in Daytona, Florida. She began with five little girls as pupils. Her capital was one dollar and fifty cents. The building was a rented cabin. The site was an old dumping ground, swampy, grown up with a jungle of underbrush. She had discovered the piece of land while exploring on her bicycle. She determined to buy the land and set to work to make the first payment. The Clarendon Hotel was being built near by on the beach at Daytona. She made potato pies and sold them to the workmen. Five dollars earned from the sale of these penny pies made the down payment on the old dump land, which had to be filled and cleared before a school could even be built.

The first building erected, a big white frame structure, was called Faith Hall. It was "prayed up, sung up, and talked up." She had taken up an impossible task: a Negro organizing and financing an institution for Negroes; but the visions of the cotton field were still hers, and an indomitable will and a mystical faith in God's sustaining help.

Today Bethune-Cookman College has buildings and

equipment valued at over one million dollars, and more than two hundred and fifty men and women who are being trained in home making, thrift, cleanliness, and good citizenship. Faculty and students reflect the spirit of the founder. The modern buildings set among the live oaks with their trailing Spanish moss are filled with youth who seem determined to redeem their people through creative work.

As I entered the college chapel I saw above the outside of the door the motto, *Enter to Learn*. And above the inside of the chapel door the words that the departing worshiper must face, *Depart to Serve*. The students came in quietly and took their places, joining in the singing of spirituals and meditative hymns. There was no leader or choir. The audience needed no exhortation. They created their own mood of worship. Through the palms outside the chapel windows came the rosy glow of a Florida sunset.

"Depart to serve" was the spirit of the college. Along with her academic work, Mary Bethune initiated extension work among the children in a turpentine camp near by, established a Negro Y.M.C.A. for the community, and was now remodeling an old building on the campus, which was to be opened as a primary school for children in the neighborhood. In the art cottage I heard the story of evening classes carried on for Negro adults. Some women were fascinated when they found that they could draw objects with a pencil. "I never knew," said one of them, "that you could make flowers like that on paper!" One woman made some curtains from unbleached muslin and put them up in her cabin. When her husband came home he was surprised. "What's dem things on de windows?"

"Curtains I made at de college."

He went out and got some paint and painted the drab interior of the cabin.

A touch of beauty had transformed the place.

Later the wife brought home a small rag rug made from old silk stockings. Seeing it on the floor, he asked what it was and she said. "It's a rug to put on de flooh."

"Dat's too nice to put on de flooh," he answered. "You let me lay heah on de cot wid dat rug ober my feet, an' you call in de neighbors and let dem see." Proudly the man of the house lay on the cot with the handiwork of his wife over his feet, while the neighbors filed in to see the creation of beauty.

Mary Bethune's cotton-field visions have come true because of her tireless and sacrificial effort. She is a large, forceful woman, full of enterprise and energy. She is a born organizer, as the Sunday-afternoon programs at the school prove. She can preside with the skill of a ring master, marshaling the little tots of Daytona, who speak their pieces and sing their songs. She still draws a crowd after thirty-five years. She watches the college band like a major, sure that every uniform is spotless and everyone in step. All white visitors are welcomed and impressed with the spirit of the college. Mrs. Bethune has served as president of the National Association of Colored Women's Clubs, president of the National Association of Teachers in Colored Schools, and president of the National Council of Negro Women. She has received the Spingarn medal and the Drexel Award for distinguished service to her race and the nation, and numerous honorary degrees. "I was always an organizer," she said to me. "Usually when there was a stick of candy to be divided, I was chosen to do the dividing. I was either captain or manager of the baseball team." She chuckled in her hearty way. "Guess I was born to boss."

Her eloquence swayed a great audience in Carnegie Hall, New York, when distinguished representatives of various national and racial groups in this country spoke before an unusual international gathering. She won first honors for her convincing apologetic on behalf of the Negro race.

In Columbia, South Carolina, the capital of her childhood state, a mass meeting of five thousand people heard her present in dramatic fashion the story of her people. Suddenly a white woman walked down the aisle and onto the platform. The audience looked on breathless. They saw the white woman throw her arms around the black woman's neck and heard her pay a tribute to Mary Bethune. She was the daughter of the man who once owned Mrs. Bethune's mother. Following the Proclamation of Emancipation, the slave-mother had continued to cook for her former master until she had saved enough to buy five acres of land. Here she built a cabin and here children were born, including the daughter who was to win the name of America's foremost Negro woman, the pioneer of a new Negro America.

Since 1936 she has been director of the National Youth Administration for Negro Youth, traveling about the country supervising the government aid given to fifty-five thousand young Negroes. She points out that youth constitute one-third of our unemployed. "One-eighth of admissions to state hospitals in 1933 were between the ages of fifteen and twenty-four. Negro youth face life today with even greater handicaps than white youth: lower economic standards, inferior educational opportunities, and health hazards. Our Negro population has grown from a million in 1900 to almost twelve million in 1930. The tenth youth in America today is black. It is high time that our country should awaken and realize that we can go forward only as we go forward *together*."

"Are relationships between whites and Negroes improving in America?" I asked.

"Unquestionably. There is better understanding and

greater respect. The Negro has now proved the rôle that he can play in our national life. We have Carver and Just in science, Hayes and Anderson in music, Walker in business, our flourishing insurance companies and commercial concerns. Where doors have been opened we are proving our capacity to produce. It has taken us all these years to get out of the shadow of dense poverty and ignorance. We were denied a chance; we had no capital to invest. Now we are beginning to launch out into productive fields.

"It is reassuring to state that the Negro worker is today an indispensable part of American agriculture and industry. His labor has built the economic empires of cotton, sugar cane and tobacco; he furnishes nearly 12 per cent of all American bread-winners; one-third of all servants, one-fifth of all farmers. In 1930, we operated one million farms and owned 750,000 homes. Negroes operate today over 22,000 business establishments with over 27 million dollars in yearly receipts. Negroes manufacture more than sixty different commodities. They spend annually for groceries over two billion dollars, a billion more for clothes, with a total purchasing power in excess of four and a half billion dollars. Negro churches have more than five million members, owning 206 million dollars worth of property and spending 43 million dollars a year. Negroes are members of legislatures in twelve states; three or more states have black judges on the bench; and a federal judge has recently been appointed to the Virgin Islands. Twenty-two Negroes have sat in Congress, and there is one member in the House at present.

"But we need to add the dark side of the picture. We ought to be realistic and face facts," she went on frankly. "Thirty-six per cent of Negro workers are in agriculture. In the ten chief cotton states, three million Negroes are dependent upon tenant farms. Among 2,000 such families in four states, the small number who received any cash money at all at the end of the year averaged about $105 for the year 1934. Between 1920 and 1930, Negroes lost almost three million acres of land they once owned, an area equal to twice the size of the state of Delaware. Of all Negro workers, another 26.6 per cent are in domestic service, generally working long hours for little pay. Negro skilled and semi-skilled workers, comprising another 18 per cent are at the mercy of the trade unions, often barred from membership and forced to 'scab' in order to work. The resultant high percentage of unemployment and irregular work at low wages results in intense economic insecurity, the natural corollaries of which are too much labor by Negro women and children, poor homes and broken families, ill health, delinquency, and crime.

"In 1930, the death rate for Negroes was 82 per cent higher than that for whites; their infant mortality rate was two-thirds higher, and their death rate from tuberculosis three times that for the white group. The life expectancy for Negroes is only 47 years as compared to 59 years for the white race. The lynching of Negroes, North and South, is still a terrifying blot upon our civilization which embarrasses us before the other nations of the world. In some sections, very few Negroes are allowed to vote, and the denial of civil liberties and segregation on public carriers and in public places humiliate Negro men, women, and children.

"Fully 80 per cent of the almost twelve million Negroes in America live in 15 southern states maintaining separate school systems. In these states, 15.1 per cent of the Negroes are today illiterate, as compared with 2.5 per cent of the whites. Over one million children, more than half the enrolment and over one-third of the total group, get into no schools at all and three-fourths of *all* Negro pupils do not get beyond the *fourth grade*."

I studied Mrs. Bethune, who was seated on the studio couch, across her attractively furnished living room. She wore a black and white suit and white shirt-waist. Her broad features gave forcefulness to her words. She possessed a natural eloquence. She closed her eyes at times as if lost in the realm of her ideas, and the words flowed forth, rhythmic and moving.

"When did you first become conscious of racial discrimination?" I asked.

"At a fairly early age I sensed the injustice of my surroundings. I saw how the white man forced me to live. I always had to go to his back door. My living quarters were wretched. He controlled me, and my people took what he handed out to them. I soon realized that I was as good as he was. I knew I could do what he did if I were given a chance. As for myself, I have never been conscious of racial prejudice. I feel at home with a Chinese, Indian, or Englishman. We are all flesh, all human beings, all the same creation!

"Today in a white man's world I cannot eat in a hotel. But I have the satisfaction of knowing that my skin is as clean as that of anyone in the hotel, that I have a shining white bathroom, that my home is spotless, and my soul is beyond such pettiness. The other day in New York City I went to keep an appointment and the elevator boy refused to carry me up to the office. He told me to use the freight elevator. I refused. 'You lump all Negroes together, don't you?' I said to him. 'They're all maids to you, I suppose. What would you think if I told you all white people were elevator boys?' The young man permitted me to ride up with him."

She closed her eyes again and spoke with the forebearance of which the developed members of her race are capable. "I meet discrimination with great pity. I feel pity in my heart for those who inflict injustice and unhappiness upon me. Sorrow comes over me because of the smallness of their souls, their failure to measure up to the Christ spirit, their blindness to what brotherhood means! I want to say to them, 'Friends, if you put yourself in my place and become black for one month, then you will have compassion.' My heart has been touched more with pity than resentment; and this has kept me from growing bitter."

"What does the Negro American want today?" I asked her.

"The Negro American wants what every other American wants—respect and justice. I want the opportunity to develop myself, a chance to unfold my abilities, the chance to grow into full womanhood. In short, the Negro wants a square deal."

"What do you think is America's greatest need?" I asked.

She answered promptly, "Economic justice and social justice, the shedding of bigotry and greed, and the taking on of a spirit of fellowship. I speak not from the standpoint of racial injection of blood, but from the standpoint of fair play—recognition of the needs of the group farthest down and the willingness to share. America today needs an extension of the humanitarian spirit. We must be awakened to the importance of giving consideration and representation to the minority groups in our country.

"America should grant equal franchise to the Negro. The only voice that is heard in a democracy is the voice of the franchise. The denial of the vote to the black American is a terrible injustice. Why do we not come together, take off our gloves, and be frank about it all? Let us face this wrong and make it right. If the Negro has done wrong, he will make amends, and should not the white man do the same? What injustices has the Negro done that he should be denied a vote? What crime has he committed? He is not the big robber, the bank destroyer, the arch-criminal. He has been loyal to the American flag and has died in the trenches for it. The unknown soldier may be a black man. A worker, a lover of peace, the Negro should be given a vote!"

"What is the Negro's contribution to American life?"

"America has lost much through ignoring the spirit of the Negro, who exemplifies the virtues of human kindness and patience. America will gain a new foothold in brotherhood through imitating the spirit of the Negro, who does not strike back at those who wrong him. The songs the Negro sang while he was driven as a slave are not songs of hatred; they are songs of love. It is almost miraculous that such spiritual guidance should come from the exploited. Like the Jews in captivity, my people produced truth out of tribulation."

Mary Bethune knows what struggle is. But she has won spiritual recompenses in her conflict with poverty and injustice. She has grown beyond prejudice.

"I believe that the Negro must save himself," she went on. "Democracy will not come in mass form, but only through the willingness of individuals to learn to live. The Negro must learn to wash his own face and hands. He must win practical skill to live. Grass is better than dust and dirt; and there can be beauty where life today is barren. We can have a clean country and a free life. The white race will not accept the Negro until he possesses the essentials of culture—until he is industrious, clean, intelligent!

"I am not discouraged about the Negro. This is the grandest day in which he has ever lived. There are greater opportunities today, although we still fight against heavy odds. We are drawing closer to our goal.

"In Berne, Switzerland, I once saw a rose garden. There were many colors of roses and among them was a black rose, rich and lustrous. The realization came to me as I looked at those flowers that all colors were destined to play their part in God's garden and in his world. Flowers of all colors need the sun and the rain. You cannot expect the black rose to bloom if it is hidden away from the sun under a rock or shut off from the rain. The black rose says, 'Give me a chance and I will play my part.'"

---

*"Reason and Truth
   Are Eternally Free":*

THOMAS MANN

THE slender young German trembled with excitement as he handed the bulky package to the post-office clerk. It was a manuscript, he blushingly admitted, hundreds of pages written in long-hand. He wrote down a valuation of one thousand marks and was chagrined to see the post-office clerk smile. He turned away with misgivings. Would the publishers laugh at his effort? He was only twenty-five. But he had been working on the novel for two and a half years. He had dreamed over its plot while he filed papers at his insurance desk, and thousands of hours of toil had gone into its pages. Would it be a failure?

When he received the publisher's reply, he was in the army, where he had been drafted for his required year of service. He was advised to cut the manuscript in half. He wrote a blunt no. The publishers decided to gamble on a thousand copies; and *Buddenbrooks* was published in 1901. A few critics spoke well of the book, and the first edition was sold in a year's time. A cheaper one-volume edition followed that suddenly became popular, and printing after printing was turned off the press. Thomas Mann was famous at twenty-six. "My mail was swollen," he wrote, "money flowed in streams, my picture appeared in the papers, a hundred pens made copy of the product of my secluded hours, the world embraced me amid congratulations and shouts of praise." Over a million copies of the book were sold in Germany, while translations appeared all over the world.

Buddenbrooks is the saga of a merchant family, with many parallels to that of the author's life, the story of four generations of middle-class Germany, their moral decline and the decadence of the old German culture and of Western civilization. Mann's father was a prosperous grain merchant in the city of Lübeck, who served as senator and mayor of the free city. His mother was the daughter of a German planter in Brazil and his Portuguese-Creole wife. He says of his mother, "She was distinctly Romantic in type, in her youth a much admired beauty, and extraordinarily musical." From her he received his love for music and his artistic nature. "My childhood was sheltered and happy," he recalls. "We five brothers and sisters grew up in a spacious and dignified house, built by my father for him and his. But the brightest hours of my youth were those summer holidays at Travemunde on the Baltic bay: with their mornings spent in bathing at the beach, their afternoons, almost as passionately loved, by the steps of the bandstand opposite the gardens of the hotel. School I loathed, and to the end failed to satisfy its demands. I despised it as a milieu; I was critical of the manners of its masters and I early espoused a sort of literary opposition to its spirit, its discipline, and its methods of training."

His father died in Thomas' fifteenth year; the business was closed; and the family moved to Munich. At nineteen he went into an insurance office to begin his business career, but he went "with the word temporary in my heart." In his desk were books by Flaubert, Zola, Heine, and Goethe, which he read furtively. He went to the university to study literature and then followed his brother to Italy for a year. In Rome he wrote short stories and started the novel that brought him sudden fame.

Marrying happily, he became the father of six children. He built a fine home in Munich and for twenty-eight years lived the life of the successful artist. In 1924 he wrote *The Magic Mountain,* the story of a tuberculosis sanitorium in the Swiss Alps where a healthy young man goes to visit a sick cousin and remains for seven years to live in a community dominated by disease. He falls prey to the malady, but at last recovers, only to face the more sinister disease of War that engulfs him. This second significant novel was an omen of success and of tragedy. In 1929 its author received the Nobel Prize for Literature, and was heralded as the greatest writer of Germany.

Then the Reichstag was burned and Dr. Mann left Germany to live for a time in Switzerland and work on his long novel about Joseph. He was incensed to see freedom violated in Germany. In 1930 he declared himself publicly for a progressive German republic, warning a huge audience against rising Naziism. He was skeptical that any good would come out of National Socialism. He restrained his condemnation, however, hoping that the excesses, beating and killing, concentration camps and persecutions, would be overcome by the better instincts of his people. He waited over two years to give Hitler a chance. Finding that he had hoped in vain, he broke his silence. When an attack was written against the men of letters who had left the fatherland, Mann replied, denouncing the Nazi leaders as enemies of Western morality and of all civilization. As a result of this condemnation he was deprived of his German citizenship. The University of Bonn informed him that his name had been removed from their records and the honorary degree previously granted had been rescinded. He replied with an eloquent appeal for human liberty.

When he was sixty-one, his career as a happy and successful artist was revolutionized. He was compelled to enter the political drama of his time. He telephoned his children in Munich and told them he was coming back home from Switzerland. They replied, "But the weather is bad here." He answered naively, "It is wretched here, too." They said, "But you can't imagine how bad it is here. It would be a real hazard to your health." He got the point. His life would be threatened if he went home. He told his children to join him in Zurich. His daughter, Erika, returned in disguise to Munich to rescue the unfinished manuscript of his Joseph novel and some of his Goethe books. On a second trip she brought out his phonograph and his collection of musical records. His home and property were confiscated by the Nazi government. He was a man without a country.

An offer came from Princeton University for a series of lectures. He decided to join the exiles in America. I visited him in his large red brick house that is surrounded by a high wall on a shaded Princeton street. In the stately hall I saw a bronze bust of this most distinguished writer of our time. The long living room was furnished in simple German style, the commanding features being a grand piano and two huge mahogany bookcases that held his complete collection of Goethe's works. The library had three windows that looked out on a quiet garden. There was a fireplace, a sofa, comfortable chairs, and bookcases reaching to the ceiling. On the heavy mahogany desk were Dr. Mann's medals that record some of the honors that have come to him, a framed letter from Hermann Sudermann, a figure from Siam, an Egyptian tomb figure crudely carved out of wood, and a few piles of manuscript stacked neatly under paper weights.

Thomas Mann at sixty-four is a slender, mild-mannered scholar, who loves his books and his family. His hair and close-cropped mustache are graying and the lines of his eyes and face bear record of the conflict of the past six years. He has a high forehead, penetrating eyes, a sharp nose. His English carries a distinct German accent and he frequently makes use of German words.

I looked at a page of manuscript on his desk done in careful, painstaking German script. He writes methodically each morning from eight-thirty until noon, completing about two pages in four hours. He then eats lunch, enjoying his meals to the full; then takes a nap and a walk, attends to correspondence, and does his reading. He is an omniverous reader. He consumed an entire library of books before he began his writing of the Joseph novels about ancient Egypt. Music is his hobby. He plays the piano and the violin. Several of his children are studying music. He loves to hear classical compositions on his victrola. Once or twice a month he goes to New York or Philadelphia to hear a symphony orchestra concert.

His exile and the anxiety of the past six years have aged him. But like Dante's, his soul has been aroused by the discipline of suffering. As he explains, "There are three periods in my life. First, I was the young artist, interested only in beauty and technique. Second, I lived in a state of pessimism, under the influence of the philosophy of Nietzsche and Schopenhauer. Third, I have entered this present period of moral awakening, of groping for the reality back of realism, of searching for the infinite truth that lies back of psychoanalysis and all our modern cleverness. For a time I was fascinated with the pessimistic and romantic conception of the universe. Life and spirit, sensuality and redemption were set over against each other.

I was a disciple of Wagner. But with riper years I have turned more and more to Goethe, a far saner model who combines the ideal with action. Until recently I felt that culture meant music and metaphysics. I crowded out everything political."

But developments in contemporary Germany proved to Dr. Mann that music and intellectualism did not save a nation from barbarism. He now believes that to be non-political results in being anti-democratic. The intelligent supporter of democracy must be an active political force. The old German tradition was quite to the contrary. Like the philosopher Schopenhauer, the German bourgeois is a genial man who is indifferent to freedom; he is subjective, conservative, and leaves politics to the other person.

"This political passivity and remoteness from democracy has frightfully avenged itself," Dr. Mann has recently pointed out. "Germany has been sacrificed to a state totalitarianism which has robbed her not only of civic but of moral freedom. If we identify democracy with the recognition that the political and social are constituent parts of the human; if we say that democracy, in defending her civil freedom, defends her ethical freedom as well; then the opposite of democracy is that theory and that fundamentally anti-human practice which makes the political dominate the whole field of human affairs to the exclusion of everything else. There is a ruthless and tragic consistency in its operations from knowing nothing but the state, thinking of nothing but power, sacrificing the human being, to sacrificing all that pertains to humanity itself and making an end of freedom once and for all. The absence of political experience on the part of the intellectual German bourgeois and his contemptuous attitude towards democracy, his scorn for freedom—which to him was nothing but libertarian cant—all this resulted in nothing less than the enslavement of the citizen to the state and to power politics. It made of his life and labor a mere function of totalitarianism, and so debased him that one asks how he can ever again hold up his head before the world."

The German citizen's disdain of democratic revolution has made him the tool of another revolution which threatens the foundations of Western civilization, "a world revolution to which no invasion of the Huns in olden times can ever be compared. The German burgher could be anti-democratic because he was ignorant. He did not know that democracy is just another name for Occidental Christianity; that politics itself is nothing but intellectual morality, without which the spirit perishes."

Once proud of being detached from political and social activities, he is now convinced of the danger of isolating art from the everyday life of the world. This conviction is made clear in the lecture which Dr. Mann gave in his coast-to-coast tour of the United States in the spring of 1938. It was called *The Coming Victory of Democracy*. He made a vigorous attack on fascism, pointing out that in the fascist state the individual counts for nothing. He is a tool of the bosses, an impersonal atom. He is forced to give everything, thought, will and action, to the monster that hovers above him; and he must serve the nation as a slave. Fascism is a mere child of the times when compared with democracy. This accounts for its youthful vigor; and also indicates that it may be short lived when measured by the values of democracy, which are established and timeless.

"Democracy is thought; but it is thought related to life and action. Democracy is that form of society which is inspired above every other with the feeling and consciousness of the dignity of man.

"Faith to believe in the coming victory of democracy must be founded upon the humanly timeless aspect of democracy, upon the unlimited powers of self-renewal which are its consequence, and upon its inexhaustible store of potential youthfulness, which is nourished by the absolute. For these are the qualities which make it possible for democracy to laugh at the boastful pretensions of the fascist dictatorships to youthfulness and future glory."

He concluded his lecture with these personal words: "I left Germany because in the Germany of today the traditional values underlying Western culture have been rejected and trodden under foot. I have made many sacrifices in order to save one thing which was denied me in Germany: freedom of thought and expression. What better use could I make of this freedom than to tell of my experience during my last years in Germany and what it taught me.

"To me the chief lesson of those years is that we must not be afraid to attempt a reform of freedom—in the conservative sense. I believe it to be the duty of every thinking man to take an active part in this task—which is tantamount to the preservation of culture—and to give freely of himself. I must regretfully own that in my younger years I shared that dangerous German habit of thought which regards life and intellect, art and politics as totally separate worlds. In those days we were all of us inclined to view political and social matters as non-essentials that might as well be entrusted to politicians. And we were foolish enough to rely on the ability of these specialists to protect our highest interests. Not long after the war, however, I recognized the threat to liberty which was beginning to take form in Germany, and almost alone among writers I warned the public to the best of my powers. When subsequently the specter became reality and National-Socialism achieved absolute power, I realized at once that I should not be able to breathe in this air, that I should have to leave my home.

"Four years ago I visited America for the first time, and since then I have come here each year. I was delighted with the atmosphere that I found here, because it was almost free of the poisons that fill the air of Europe—because here, in contrast to the cultural fatigue and inclination to barbarism prevalent in the Old World, there exists a joyful respect for culture, a youthful sensitivity to its values and its products. I feel that the hopes of all those, who cherish democratic sentiments in the sense in which I have defined them, must be concentrated on this country. Here it will be possible—here it *must* be possible—to carry out those reforms of which I have spoken; to carry them out by peaceful labor, without crime and bloodshed. It is my own intention to make my home in your country, and I am convinced that if Europe continues for a while to pursue the same course as in the last two decades, many good Europeans will meet again on American soil. I believe, in fact, that for the duration of the present European dark age, the center of Western culture will shift to America. America has received much from Europe, and that debt will be amply repaid if, by saving our traditional values from the present gloom, she can preserve them for a brighter future that will once again find Europe and America united in the great tasks of humanity."

Thomas Mann was deeply affected by the Nazi seizure of Austria and Czechoslovakia. He expressed himself in strong terms: "It is one of the foulest pages in history, this story of the betrayal of the Czechoslovak Republic by European democracy; this offering up of an allied and loyal state upon the altar of fascism. . . ."

The plot against Czechoslovakia was engineered, he pointed out, by an international clique who betrayed the people of Europe. They claimed that they had averted war for the good of mankind. In reality, the leaders of the democratic powers did not dare stand against fascism; they feared that it might be replaced by a socialist revolution that would increase Russian dominance in Europe.

If the democracies had taken a bold stand against Hitler he would have played out his hand. The German people would not have supported him; and the Nazi regime would have collapsed. This was Mann's position before the invasion of Poland. I believe he still holds to it. The democracies failed at the crucial moment when they should have united in resistance to Nazi aggression.

There is no wavering with Thomas Mann. He is convinced of the truth of his position. "To be against Hitler," he says, "is always to be right. We must have no fear. Reason and truth may suffer apparent eclipse. But in us, in our hearts, they are eternally free. And looking down from the bright regions of art, the spirit may laugh at the triumphant folly of the hour. Not forsaken and alone, but secure in the bond uniting it with all that is best on earth.

"Peace has no traffic with unfreedom and lying, from them she cannot spring. She stands on the side of freedom and sincerity, she is indeed but another name for them, just as violence is but another name for unfreedom and deception.

"I feel a sort of shame and yet withal a strange joyousness as I utter these moralizing words," he wrote in *This Peace,* "That joy would have been foreign to my early years. Any cultured mind would have felt contempt for such truths, they would have seemed trivial and unworthy to the subtle and sceptical sense. But the position of mind has strangely altered upon this earth. An epoch of reaction has set in, of lawlessness and moral anarchy. And yet, paradoxical as it may sound, the *spirit* has at the same time entered into a new age of *morality*. I mean an age of simplification, of humble recognition of the distinction between good and evil. Yes, once more we are aware, once more we know good and evil. Evil has been revealed to us with such crassness and vulgarity that our eyes are opened to the dignity and simple beauty of the good. We have taken it to heart and feel that it does not do any harm to our 'finesse' to confess it.

"That is, if you like, a renewal of the spirit. And indeed I have often thought that such an epoch of spiritual renewal and simplification might be America's great hour. I have said that in this dark age it would be her task to preserve and administer the cultural inheritance of the Western world. What I had in mind was this: her youth, her unexhausted moral freshness; her mental temper, which stands closer to the Biblical and monumental than any in Europe, fit her, at this crisis in world affairs, to lift her voice with simple and massive authority. There would be nothing in this of presumption, but of independence and freedom, which have become a moral necessity for this country, and which may help towards the spiritual healing of Europe too. In a desolate and morally leaderless world, may America stand the strong and unswerving protectress of the good and the godlike in man. May she do this in the knowledge of good and evil, aware of her own human insufficiency, but scorning violence and the lie, and standing by her sound and vital belief in the good, in freedom and truth, peace and justice."

The tumult of events since 1933 has transformed Mann from a conservative burgher and a wealthy artist into an ardent champion of human liberty. With this prophetic crusade has come an inner rebirth. He now feels that nineteenth-century liberalism has been outgrown. The twentieth century will witness the rebirth of a new religion. This new religion will lift us from our cynicism and contempt for the human race by giving us new faith in man. In spite of the evidence of humanity's vileness we should remember man's honorable traits revealed in art, science, and justice. We need to remember the infinite mystery that lies back of humanity.

"This new humanism will not flatter mankind, looking at it through rose-colored glasses, for it will have had experiences of which preceding humanisms did not know. It will have stout-hearted knowledge of man's dark, daemonic, radically 'natural' side, united with reverence for his super-biological, spiritual worth. The new humanism will be universal, and it will have the artist's attitude; that is, it will recognize that the immense value and beauty of the human being lies precisely in the fact that he belongs to the two kingdoms of nature and spirit. It will realize that no romantic conflict or tragic dualism is inherent in the fact, but rather a fruitful and engaging combination of determinism and free choice. Upon that it will base a love for humanity in which its pessimism and its optimism will cancel each other."

His epic story of Joseph, which has become his life work, chooses as its central character a man "blest with blessing from the heavens above and from the depths beneath." In this blessing spoken by Jacob over his son, Joseph, Dr. Mann expresses his formula for an ideal humanity. In humanity there are both darkness and light, the primitive and the civilized, despair and hope. The new religion is not all sweetness and light, nor is it all despair and darkness. It binds us to human suffering and also offers us hope to meet our duty.

Perhaps the distinguished writer will present his complete and final philosophy in the last volume of the long Joseph novel. Here he portrays his ideal character, a conception that may rise above the low estimate of the individual that prevails in our dictator-dominated world. The third volume, published in 1936, left Joseph in prison. He had not won his way through to freedom. Significantly, the book was concluded in the third year of its author's exile, in a period when he was less sure of the collapse of fascism than he is today. To some extent Joseph may become the expression of the spiritual regeneration that he believes essential to the recovery of mankind.

Thomas Mann stands among civilization's great champions of liberty. He has given up home and property, sacrificed high standing in the fatherland, and become an exile because of his love for freedom. It stirs our jaded and pessimistic age to contemplate the tonic vigor of his belief. Amid the anarchy of our time the spirit of man is slowly emerging into renaissance. We are at last being aroused to the sinister evils of prejudice and violence. We are beginning to appreciate the priceless value of truth and right. We can and must reassert ourselves morally to redeem civilization from barbarism, and stand in an ethically leaderless world as the protectors of the good and the godly!

First Woman of the Orient:

MADAME CHIANG KAI-SHEK

THE bright-eyed little Chinese girl never dreamed, as she played beneath the old trees on the Georgia college campus, that she was destined to become the most influential woman in the world. Her father had been brought to the United States by his uncle, a silk and tea merchant. Young Charles Soong wanted to remain and go to school in the fascinating new country, but his uncle refused to give his consent. The boy ran away, determined in his plans. He served as cabin boy on a steamer that ran from Boston to Savannah. While in the South he was baptized, taking the name of his religious sponsor, captain of the *Colfax*, in which he arrived from the island of Hainan in 1880. General Julian Carr of Durham took an interest in Charles Soong and sent him to Trinity College, now Duke University. In 1885 he received a theological certificate from Vanderbilt University.

Returning to China, he became a teacher and a publisher of Christian literature. He married a woman who was actively interested in religion, who was to prove a wife of shrewdness and ability. Charles Soong brought his family to the United States, living for a time in Summit, New Jersey, and then in Macon, Georgia. He placed his three lovely daughters: Ching-ling, Ai-ling and Mei-ling on the campus of Georgia Wesleyan College. The two older girls following the college course, while Mei-ling studied under tutors. When the family moved back to China, Mei-ling was sent to Wellesley College, where she was both popular and a brilliant student. She was the first Oriental student to win the Wellesley and Durant scholarships. Meanwhile, her father had become a successful publisher and business man and was accumulating a fairly substantial fortune.

The Wellesley graduate returned to her homeland to begin a careful study of the Chinese classics and to engage in social work. She was appointed a member of a Child Labor Commission to investigate labor conditions in the industries of the foreign settlement in Shanghai. She was the first Chinese woman to be asked to serve in such a capacity. For ten years Mei-ling interested herself in cultural affairs, social reform, and enjoyed the cosmopolitan life of Shanghai. Her sister, Ching-ling, married Dr. Sun Yat-sen, the leader of the Chinese revolution. Her sister, Ai-ling, married Dr. H. H. Kung, a direct descendant of Confucius, and a wealthy business man and prominent politician. Her brother, T. V. Soong, forged ahead and became an outstanding political leader. Mei-ling moved among the leaders of the New China, and was known as the belle of Shanghai.

In 1927 Chiang Kai-shek made a proposal of marriage. *Who's Who in China* for 1925 does not mention the name of Chiang Kai-shek. One year later he was leading the southern armies on their successful expedition to the north for the unification of China. Two years later he was the outstanding military man in the country. Three years later he was head of the government. Born of humble parentage, in 1887, Chiang proved a poor student. His widowed mother sacrificed to keep him in school, but he did not get along with his fellow students. They bullied him and he resented it. He disgusted his relatives by running away and joining the army. The military profession had always been considered the lowest occupation by the Chinese. At eighteen he took the examination for the new military school established in Paotingfu; and surprised everyone by winning first place.

His mother arranged for his marriage when he was about sixteen to a girl he had never seen. After the ceremony the couple paid their accustomed call on the bride's parents. Chiang, eager to please, had brought along a company of actors to furnish entertainment. The village people frowned on theatricals. The father-in-law was disgusted. The groom was told to leave the house. He went; and never forgave his father-in-law. He lived with his first wife for only a short time; and obtained a divorce in 1921. After the military academy there were four years of study in Japan. The island kingdom was stirring with new life after the victory over Russia. Numerous Chinese revolutionists were studying and planning in Japan. In 1910 Chiang heard a stirring address by the revolutionist, Dr. Sun Yat-sen. He was enthusiastic, and determined to enlist in the cause.

During the Revolution of 1911 Chiang was given command of a regiment. He made model soldiers of his men, revealing his passion for order and efficiency. The revolution received many set-backs. In 1916 Chiang was a penniless clerk in Shanghai, buying his food from itinerant street vendors. He became an exchange broker. During the World War he made money and established contact with influential friends. He saved Sun Yat-sen's life in 1922, when a hostile war lord attacked him. He convinced Sun of the need of organizing a strong military force in order to carry the revolution through to success. Russia offered her help in carrying on the revolution. Dr. Sun sent Chiang to study in Russia for a year. In 1923, Russian advisors and military instructors were flooding China. Sun said, "We no longer look to the West; we now look to Russia."

Chiang agreed. He, too, was convinced that Russia was the only country that was willing to help China. He undertook the reorganization of Whampoa Military Academy and made it the center of China's revolutionary cause. He trained youth to think in terms of their country. Dr. Sun learned to count more and more on his capable young associate. Soon after Sun's death, Chiang assumed command of the Nationalist army. He was beginning by this time to question the value of communist leadership. The Marxist program did not fit China's needs. Their violence and terrorism were disrupting the life of the nation. In 1927, General Chiang turned against the Communists and stated that they should leave China. Because of a division due to difference of opinion, he resigned his position as commander-in-chief. He left for Japan to await change of events in China; and also to propose to Mei-ling. He had met her five years before in Shanghai, and was deeply impressed by her brilliant intellect and beauty.

Mother Soong was a woman of remarkable character. Chiang respected her; and her religious faith was to exert a profound effect upon him during the next few years. She asked him if he were ready to become a Christian. He answered that he would not become a Christian in order to win the hand of her daughter, but that he would be glad to study the new religion open-mindedly. Mother Soong was impressed with his sincerity. She gave him a Bible and asked him to read it. Meanwhile, he won the consent of Mei-ling as he outlined his plans for a new China and for their life together. The family soon fell into line.

The marriage took place in Shanghai at the close of 1927. Nine days later the government asked Chiang to resume office as generalissimo, and also to serve as chairman of the National Military Council. He returned to leadership with greater authority than he had had at his resignation. But there were grave problems: China was torn by civil strife; communists were fighting non-communists; rival war lords were battling to extend their control. The hopeless turmoil had been in process for seventeen years; and there seemed no prospect of a solution. The war lords Feng and Yen opposed Chiang's efforts at national unification. His war with them left him worn, nervous, and sick at heart. The Generalissimo carried the Bible that his mother-in-law had given him and read it while at the front. During cold nights on the lonely north-western plains he found solace in the new religion. It brought peace and the faith that he could create a new China.

Immediately after her marriage Madame Chiang began to take an active part in national affairs. Her first interest was social welfare. She inaugurated the movement for the establishment of the Officers' Moral Endeavor Society, a sort of Chinese military Y.M.C.A. She established schools in Nanking for the children of revolutionary heroes. Here five hundred boys and three hundred girls, descendants of

Kuomintang veterans, are prepared to serve their country. Students are taught modern methods of agriculture; they operate a farm and dairy. The boys learn carpentery, plastering, canning, and carpet-making; the girls learn sewing, weaving, cooking, and various hand crafts. The older students conduct rural service projects, health clinics, and farm welfare schools.

She encouraged the formation of clubs for women throughout the country. She began to write articles on the new spirit of China for publication in China, Europe, and the United States. She became a member of the Legislative Department, an assistant in the program of the National Economic Reconstruction Movement. As secretary-general of the National Aviation Commission she has helped in the reorganization of China's air forces. More than all this, she is a partner in the government. Every important question receives her consideration and judgment. She is almost constantly with her husband; and has become his chief advisor. With her social grace and fluent English she has become his foreign liaison officer, welcoming foreign visitors, interpreting for him, and translating his addresses and manifestoes. Each day she gives him a digest of world news. She has introduced him to Western literature and Western music. Chiang had the possibilities of a great leader before he married Mei-ling; but certainly the marriage has made him a greater man. No woman in the world today holds a position comparable with that of Madame Chiang.

The Generalissimo's stand against communism brought disaster to him and to the country; but it now begins to appear that it was the wise stand to take, considering the future of China. There were bloody combats; vast areas were laid waste; thousands of lives were lost. Chiang was convinced that Sun Yat-sen's principles could not be reconciled with those of Karl Marx. He believed that

China's future revolution must be carried out along the line of the *Kuomintang* program, and not that of the Bolsheviks. He knew that communism was strongly entrenched in China and that it had something to offer his people. He came to see that the power of communism could not be uprooted through military force. A new social and economic program would have to be launched to educate and win the people.

The result was the joint creation of Generalissimo and Madame Chiang, the New Life Movement, which was launched in the capital of Kiangsi in 1934.

"The general psychology of our people today can be described in one word—spiritlessness," said Chiang. "What manifests itself in behavior is this: no discrimination between the good and the evil, no difference between what is public and what is private, and no distinction between the fundamental and the expedient. Because there is no discrimination between the good and the evil, consequently right and wrong are confused; because there is no difference between public and private, there lacks proper guidance for taking and giving; and because there is no distinction between the fundamental and the expedient, there is misplacement of the first and the last. As a result, officials tend to be dishonest and avaricious; the masses are undisciplined and calloused; the adults are ignorant and corrupt; the youth become degraded and intemperate; the rich become extravagant and luxurious; and the poor become mean and disorderly. Naturally, it resulted in the complete disorganization of social order and national life. Consequently, we are not in a position either to prevent or to remedy natural calamities or disasters caused from within or invasions from without. The individual, society, and the whole country are now suffering. It would be impossible even to continue living under such miserable conditions. It is, therefore, absolutely necessary to get rid of these backward conditions and to start to lead a new and rational life."

The New Life Movement encourages the industrious and Spartan life, good habits of personal appearance, and the observance of the traditional Chinese virtues. The four virtues emphasized were: *Li,* which means regulated attitudes, behavior; *I,* which means right conduct, justice; *Lien,* which means clear discrimination, integrity; *Ch'ih,* which means self-respect and honor.

Eight principles were outlined:

1. "Regard yesterday as a period of death, today a period of life. Let us rid ourselves of old abuses, and build up a new nation.
2. Let us accept the heavy responsibilities of serving the nation.
3. Let us observe rules, have faith, honesty, and humility.
4. Let us keep our clothing, eating, living, and traveling habits simple, orderly, plain, and clean.
5. Face hardships willingly; strive for frugality.
6. Acquire adequate knowledge and have moral integrity as citizens.
7. Let our actions be courageous and rapid.
8. Let us act on our promises; or, better, act without promising."

Madame Chiang became director of the Women's Division of the New Life Movement. She said, "The work of the New Life Movement is proving to be the first stage of a long battle against ignorance, dirt, carelessness, unsuitable dwellings, and the corruption that has for so long cost so much in human suffering.

"Cleanliness and neatness, (e.g., the proper use of a handkerchief, the buttoning of one's gown or uniform when out of doors) are strictly enjoined. It is no common thing for city officials, from the mayor downwards, to be seen sweeping the streets as an example to the people generally, and in scores of towns a sanitation inspector pays a weekly visit to every house, and affixes a label marked 'Clean,' 'Fairly Clean,' or 'Dirty.' But the suppression of opium, of official corruption, of dishonesty in business dealings are also in the forefront of the Movement's program, and though we recognize that men are not made sober, nor honest, nor virtuous by acts of parliament, yet if the rulers of China practise what they preach something, at least, of permanent value may be accomplished."

Those who know China realize that achieving any social change is a colossal task. The New Life Movement was an ambitious undertaking, although commendable and sorely needed. The movement spread rapidly. A monster clean-up campaign was held in Nanking. Cities and towns launched drives to halt cigarette smoking, spitting, and the littering of public places with watermelon seed. In some localities a new orderliness was noticeable on trains, buses, and boats. Trains started on time; third-class carriages were kept as clean as those of first class. Social disorder was reduced. Service corps went about the country advocating reforestation in the spring, public health activities in the summer, thrift education in the fall, and famine and other relief work in the winter. Thousands of volunteers enlisted in these service corps.

New Life headquarters organized the Chinese Association for the Prevention of Blindness and Justice to the Blind; and took the lead in war relief during the Japanese invasion, forming the Women's War Service Association, the War Orphan's Relief Committee, and many other humane agencies.

The Chiangs realized that one of the chief evils of China was graft. Every official was collecting some form of "squeeze." There was no moral stigma connected with grafting. They brought groups of officials to Nanking and informed them that graft must be stopped—that China was entering a new era. The Generalissimo went to Szechuan, which was probably the worst-governed province. Taxes had been collected from the exploited peasants years in advance. The people had been bled by years of civil war. Communists were gaining headway. Chiang announced that official corruption must come to an end; that military men must keep out of politics, courts, and business. The opium evil had to be faced. The poppy had supported armies and officials for centuries. He inaugurated a control program that was to lead to gradual suppression.

Not all of the Chiang reforms have succeeded. The average American reader cannot grasp the obstacles to change that exist in an ancient country such as China with such vast area, division by dialect, and almost total illiteracy. We must give the Chiangs credit for possessing the resolution to remain at the head of a government constantly threatened by collapse and weakened by almost every conceivable difficulty. They have proved to be the first leaders since the revolution who have sufficient stamina to stay with the job.

In 1936 the Generalissimo was kidnaped at Sian and imprisoned for thirteen days. Marshal Chang Hsueh-liang and his associates seized him because they demanded a stronger foreign policy, and an aggressive stand against Japan. The country was stirred by Japan's invasion of Manchuria and Shanghai. Chiang felt that China did not dare undertake a war against Japan. He believed in watchful waiting. While at Sian he was attacked. Almost all of his loyal bodyguard were killed and he himself was injured.

Madame Chiang and her brother, T. V. Soong, flew to Sian in an effort to save the Generalissimo, and to avert attack by the government forces. During the captivity

Chiang conducted himself with heroism. He refused to compromise with those who clamored for war or to commit the government. He had decided that he would never escape and had resigned himself to death. He urged the rebels to shoot him if they would not release him unconditionally. "If I make any pledges to gain my own release," he argued, "I should be a contemptible coward and should deserve to be killed."

His captors got hold of Chiang's diary, read it, and were affected by these words:

"I know that these rebels are very dangerous people. I am determined to fight them with moral character and spiritual strength, and with the principles of righteousness. When I was young I studied the classics of our sages. After I attained manhood I devoted myself to the revolutionary cause. There are many heroic deeds in our history. The martyrs of the former ages always defied death. Being a great admirer of these heroes, I prefer to follow in their footsteps instead of disgracing myself. The courageous life as taught by the late Sun Yat-sen should be followed by us all. Unless we do this calamity will certainly overtake us all. Jesus Christ was tempted by Satan and withstood him for forty days. He fought against evil influences more strongly than I do today. I am now, however, fighting the mutineers with ever-increasing moral strength. I must maintain the same spirit which led Jesus Christ to the Cross, and I must be ready to meet any death which the mutineers may bring upon me by the so-called 'people's judgment.'"

Chang Hsueh-liang was touched by the journal of his prisoner. He said to him, "We have read your diary and from them we have learned the greatness of your personality, your loyalty to the revolutionary cause, and your determination to bear the responsibility of saving the country far exceed anything we could have imagined."

On the fourteenth day he was permitted to return by plane to Nanking. The whole nation celebrated his release. The Sian episode won him the admiration of the people and increased his popularity. His long hours of suffering and fear had caused him to study his Bible and to become an even stronger Christian. "The greatness and love of Christ burst upon me with a new inspiration, increasing my strength to struggle against evil, to overcome temptation, and to uphold righteousness," he stated. During the attack at Sian his back had been seriously injured. He refused to rest until physicians insisted that he would become an invalid for life if he did not go to the hospital.

Soon after this hospital experience came Japan's ruthless invasion with terror, bloodshed, desolation such as China had never known in all her sorrows. The hopeful activities of the New Life Movement were suddenly brought to an end. Mass education, health, road building, farm projects were forgotten in the desperate effort to bury the dead, nurse the wounded, evacuate crowds from bombed and burning cities, and provide for millions of orphans and refugees. Generalissimo and Madame Chiang have carried the overwhelming burden of more than two years of war with a courage that has won the admiration of the world. They have watched Shanghai, Nanking, and Hankow reduced to shambles by a barbarism that surpasses any of the bloody annals of war. They moved westward, deserting one capital after another until they reached Chungking in the far west. All along the way they witnessed the sorry debacle of harried millions driven from their homes, fleeing from the relentless enemy.

Madame Chiang led the women of China into the hospitals to care for the wounded, took upon herself the care of the war orphans, and has given herself tirelessly in the effort to relieve the overwhelming suffering about her. She has flown from province to province, helping plan

China's defense, and organizing relief. She persuaded the directors of the largest cotton mill in Wuchang to remove their machinery and their thousands of factory operators to the interior. They had refused to move because they were making money; they did not care how many of their workers were bombed. She went to the factory at five o'clock in the morning, saw the conditions under which the girls worked, and shamed the management into being more humane and patriotic.

She wrote before the fall of Hankow, "There is one bright hope emerging from the gloom of apparent bankruptcy of statesmanship, however. That is the determination of the people of civilized nations to do something themselves to lessen by boycott the power and opportunities of Japan to continue with her terrible debauchery in China. A further hope is that the voice of the women can be raised to try to stop the mental and moral demoralization that seems to have descended like a disease upon the statesmen of the world. I urge womankind to speak with no uncertainty to save our innocent people and to insure the future of those of other lands. If that cannot be done then the infamies that are happening in China, will, in time, surely happen in your and other countries. Millions of our people have been bombed and burned out of their homes; hundreds of thousands of non-combatants have been slain by bombs, by bullets, and by bayonets, in cold blood; thousands of women and girls have been treated with brutality unpermissible of description. Accounts of the barbarity of the Japanese troops wherever they have penetrated into China would be unbelievable were their actions not confirmed and vouched for by independent foreign observers."

Then she adds, "If we all stand together now in confidence and in faith, surely the Japanese never can conquer us. I am sure they cannot. I realize their strength, and

I do not boast. We are bound to suffer terribly, but we will not spill our blood or sacrifice our lives in vain. China will come out of this trial a nation with a soul, marching upon the highway to greatness. That is inevitable.

"I am much discouraged at times," she confesses, "but I believe it is the spirit of persistence and self-sacrifice which will eventually regenerate China. And the regeneration of China is coming, no matter what happens!"

When they are not traveling today the Chiangs are in Chungking, the Szechuan capital built on the hills far up the Yangtze. The long and disastrous war has matured them both, deepened their spirit of devotion and their determination to save China. They have simplified life. They entertain only to undertake some highly important project; they leave social activities for the foreign office. Meals are restricted to four principal dishes, which is a rigorous curtailment in a country where a modest dinner runs to fifteen courses. Moreover, each guest is expected to fill his own rice bowl, a self-help gesture that would have been considered a distinct loss of face a few years ago. At one time the Chiangs served wine for their guests, taking grape juice themselves. Today there is no wine. Temperance and frugality are their household slogan.

The Generalissimo seems tall for a Chinese, although he is only five feet eight. He is lithe and slender. His delicate hands do not look like those of a soldier. His gray hair and mustache are close-cropped. He still looks youthful at fifty-two, efficient and energetic. His penetrating eyes study his interviewer, while he comes directly to the point. Chinese consider him brusque because he is impatient with palavering. He is quick tempered, and demands that things get done. He personally owns several planes and always travels by air. There is nothing of the rabble-rouser about him. He is retiring, avoids public functions, seldom speaks at rallies or over the air. The simple Sun Yat-sen uniform of gray or olive drab is his usual costume. For dress he wears a long Chinese gown with a black silk jacket. He supports a school of one thousand students, which he built in the town where he was born.

At forty-seven Madame Chiang is a graceful figure, always well dressed, friendly and vivacious, the epitome of Oriental beauty. But underneath her social grace is one consuming purpose: service to China. She is quite American in her manner, full of energy, and constantly tempted to overwork. The crisis of the war has made her more religious. "Many people say they believe in this thing and that, and disbelieve in other things," she writes. "My answer has been and is that you cannot change anything unless you change man's character. This means teaching people to love others as you love yourself—that is the heart of it all."

Every morning the entire Chiang household pauses for Bible reading and prayer. It makes no difference where they are: in the air, on the battlefield, in the country, or the capital. All work ceases; all guests wait. For a few minutes there is silence and meditation. The Generalissimo's captivity at Sian and the heartbreaking burdens of the war have made him a more confirmed Christian. Madame Chiang, too, says that she has also come into a new experience of God.

When Japan invaded Manchuria she went to her mother and said, "Mother, you know how to pray. Why don't you pray that God should send an earthquake or some terrible calamity upon the Japanese people to rebuke them for this wrong." Her old mother was silent for a moment. Then she answered, "You should know better, my dear, than to make such a request of God." Her mother's rebuke gave her a new attitude of forgiveness toward her enemy. She was determined to pray with the same forgiving spirit.

There have been three spiritual periods in her life since her marriage, she says. At first she was consumed with a passionate desire to do something for the country. The opportunity was before her. With her husband she could work ceaselessly to make China strong. She flung herself into many activities. "I had the best of intentions. But something was lacking. There was no staying power. I was depending on myself."

Then came the second phase: the Japanese invasion, the collapse of all reform, the death of her mother. "I was plunged into dark despair. A terrible depression settled over me—spiritual despair, bleakness, desolation. At the time of my mother's death the blackness was greatest. A foreign foe was on our soil in the north. A discontented political faction in the south. A famine in the north-west. Floods threatening the millions who dwell in the Yangtze valley. And my beloved mother taken from us. What was left?

"And then I realized that spiritually I was failing my husband. My mother's influence on the General had been tremendous. His own mother was a devout Buddhist. It was my mother's influence and personal example that had led him to become a Christian. Too honest to promise to be one just to win her consent to our marriage, he had promised my mother that he would study Christianity and read the Bible. And I suddenly realized that he was sticking to his promise, even after she was gone, but losing spiritually because there were so many things he did not understand. In common parlance, I have 'to hand it to him' for sticking to his daily Old Testament reading when without illumination there was little help in it for him.

"I began to see that what I was doing to help, for the sake of the country, was only a substitute for what he needed. I was letting him head toward a mirage when I knew of the oasis. Life was all confusion. I had been in the depths of despair. Out of that, and the feeling of human inadequacy, I was driven back to my mother's God.

I knew there was a power greater than myself. I knew God was there. But mother was no longer here to help the General spiritually, and in helping him I grew spiritually myself.

"Thus I entered into the third period, where I wanted to do, not my will, but God's. Life is really simple, and yet how confused we make it. In old Chinese art, there is just one outstanding object, perhaps a flower, on a scroll. Everything else in the picture is subordinated to that one beautiful thing. An integrated life is like that. What is that one flower? As I feel now, it is the will of God. But to know His will, and do it, calls for absolute sincerity and honesty. Political life is full of falsity and diplomacy and expediency. My firm conviction is that one's greatest weapon is not more deceptive falsity, more subtle diplomacy, greater expediency, but the simple, unassailable weapons of sincerity and truth."

There are some who distrust Chiang's Christianity, feeling that he may be using it as a bid for Western sympathy in China's crisis; but those who know him and have been in his home are convinced of his sincerity. His position as head of an army does place him somewhat in the position of an Oliver Cromwell; and his record as a soldier cannot be altogether blameless. But his growth during the past few years indicates a development that may vindicate some of his former failures. If Japan fails in her war of aggression, if China is aroused to co-operate and rebuild after the pattern of the Chiang program, we may witness a phenomenal rebirth, and the Chiangs may rise to still greater influence.

Today they go about amid the jostling crowds in the tunnels that are being dug in the hills of Chungking. There are daily air raids between nine in the morning and two in the afternoon. The administrative offices are opened in the late afternoon and are busy late into the night. The ancient, backward city with its steep, winding streets is teeming with refugees, soldiers and government officials. An unparalleled revolution is in process. New roads, telephone lines, radio stations, and public buildings are being erected amid the dynamite blast and the sharp sound of chisels on stone as the tunnels stretch back into the city hills. The intense activity is punctuated by air raid sirens, the crash of bombs, the scurry of crowds, and the patrol of ambulance corps. Vast areas of the west are still untouched by the Japanese. Today they are stirring with new life. Throughout the world's largest republic loyalty to China's cause and to the Chiangs has grown instead of lessening. Today this couple guides the destinies of a nation greater in population than all Europe combined. They have aroused in their people a faith to believe and to endure. Perhaps enemy planes will one day circle over the smoking ruins of Chungking. The Chiangs may play the rôle of Haile Selassie, and imperialism may again be victorious. But, on the other hand, they may build one of the mightiest nations in history.

The Lure of the Impossible:

CHEVALIER JACKSON

A BURLY, half-drunken Negro was beating a team of four horses hitched to a heavily loaded coal wagon that was mired in the mud. Roaring curses, he lashed his bleeding team. With each savage onslaught the horse that was hit lunged against his collar; but the animals were too frightened to pull together. They were up to their stomachs in mud, and the wagon was mired axle-deep. In the crowd that had collected on both sides of the road was a thin little boy. Tears were streaming down his face. He pleaded with the Negro to unload his coal on a platform of rails. "We will all help you unload," he shouted, expecting the crowd to co-operate.

The Negro glared at him through his bleary eyes and, shaking his black-snake whip, shouted, "Hey, you damned skinny little houn' cry-baby, 'f yuh don' shet up an' git the hell out o' here I'll cutcha in two." The lad crouched back from the whip that snapped viciously toward him. The crowd started to carry rails from the roadside fence. They were going to heed his wishes. No, they were making a narrow platform beside each horse. A man took his place on each platform with a hickory coal-pick handle and began beating the horse beside him.

Sobbing, and faint with the horror of the scene, young Chevalier Jackson started running for home. His father would do something about it. He had been a veterinarian; and knew how to handle horses and men. The first hill was steep; and the boy fell exhausted as he crossed the ridge. At least he was out of hearing of the cursing and lashing. After a few moments of rest he ran home, told his father what had happened; and rushed to the haymow to hide until he could stop his sobbing.

The frail and sensitive boy spent a wretched boyhood in the Pennsylvania mining town. He could not bear to see human beings or animals suffer. The coal miners were fond of cock fighting. The delicate, needlelike steel spurs, made by skilled toolmakers, were fastened on the cock's legs. Fights would be staged summer evenings and winter Sundays. Chevalier despised the brutality. When he saw a fight he would run away and hide until it was over. Once he dashed into the ring and tried to break up the contest. A miner seized him by the collar, shook and kicked him, and then flung him on the manure heap. "Spoil a bit o' sport, will ye?" he snarled. "Now git out o' hyur, ye cry baby, ur I'll break every bone in yer damn lil' body."

He hated dog fights, fist fights among boys, especially the prize fights that were glorified by the miners. It was not danger that threatened him and made him cry; it was the indescribable suffering of living things that he seemed helpless to relieve.

His school days were a nightmare of persecution and torment. He was a small, delicate boy, but clever at drawing and creating things with his hands, and one of the best students in the school. Boys twice his size and age "got even" by means of their bullying. On the way to school they would pull off his cowhide boots, fill them with snow and toss them over the fence. By the time the boots were recovered and emptied of their slush his feet were nearly frozen; and they would remain cold and wet all day. The boys would strip the drawings he had painstakingly prepared out of the geography book and smear them with mud. On the way home he would be waylaid and beaten. They would hold him by the feet and then swing him round and round until he would fall with vertigo when released. Another torture was to choke him. They would threaten, "Now we're going to kill you. You'll never see your mother again."

One winter he worked for days to build a sled; and it was a success, light and fast. When he went to school, the sled attracted attention as it stood against the wall of the coal-shed among the rough, poorly made sleds of the other boys. After school his prize was missing. A long search led him to a pile of splintered wood tied with his sled cord. It was on the woodpile. Under the cord on a dirty piece of paper were these words, crudely printed: "Kindlin' Wood."

One day school was dismissed at noon because the plaster fell off the ceiling. Chevalier was eager to get home to work in his shop. "I was hurrying homeward," he writes, "when suddenly I was seized from behind by powerful unseen hands; my cap was pulled down over my eyes, blindfolding me. Another pair of hands seized me, tied my hands and feet together behind my back, and I was carried off. By the cool, damp, peculiar odor of the air I realized I was being carried into a coal pit. There were a number of pit mouths: some were in use, others were for drainage, still others had been abandoned; they were here and there along the way, a little back from the edge of the road. It seemed like a long time in the mine before I was dropped into a puddle of cold water. I heard footsteps hurrying away; then all was silent, except for the drip, drip, drip of water. Not a word had been said by my captors at any time. The cap slipped off my eyes, but I could see nothing in the absolute darkness. My feet and hands had not been tied tightly; the slimy mud enabled me after a time to slip out first one hand, then the other. Taking the boots off enabled me to slip off the loops on my ankles along with the boots and stockings. Then I felt my eyes; they seemed all right, but I could not see anything. Fumbling in the dark, I separated the cold wet stockings from the loops of cord and put them on; then emptied the boots of water and put them on. I was soaking wet and shivering with the cold; my fingers were numb.

"Getting to my feet I bumped my head against the slate. This showed me that I must be in one of the worked-out rooms of the mine where the coal ribs and props had been taken out to let the room cave in. I knew I could walk upright in the working part of a mine. I felt sure that if I groped along touching one wall I could come into the main entry and see daylight. But there must have been a labyrinth of worked-out rooms. Turning corner after corner, I got to no entry with a gleam of daylight nor any passage where I could stand erect. Many times the headroom grew less and less—by which it was evident I was going wrong, because my captors must have had headroom to walk so briskly when carrying me. No sound of voices or picks or of barking draft dogs came to my ears. All was silent except the dripping water. I realized I was lost in old abandoned workings. But I kept on and on. The footing was bad; loose slate piles alternated with pools of cold mine water and slimy, slippery mud. Often I stumbled or slipped and fell. I was getting very tired. More and more often I sat on a slate pile to rest and listen. Becoming weaker and weaker, chilled and shivering, I kept on until after a hard fall I was so tired that even the slate pile seemed restful. Whether I fainted from exhaustion or fell asleep, and for how long I was unconscious, I never knew. I felt something cold on my face; then hot breath on my nose and a hot, rough tongue licking my cheek. My hand touched leather on a woolly hide, and I knew it was a harnessed pit dog that was standing over me. Then I heard a far-away shout, 'Come on huyr, Jack. Where be ye, anyways? Damn ye, come on, Jackanapes!' The cursing voice was getting farther and farther away, and then it faded out. I tried to cry out, but my voice was so weak I could scarcely hear myself. Jack stopped licking my face and let a bark out of him. Then the barking became almost incessant, with a few licks in between."

The miner at last crawled in. It was huge Welch Davy, the champion prize-fighter. He carried "Chev" to his kindly wife, who got dry clothes on him. Two sisters from the Catholic church moved him home in a covered wagon. He was desperately ill with pneumonia. For two weeks recovery seemed impossible. This long illness was to weaken his lungs and cause serious trouble later on.

Chev was ambitious and active. He did not care for

games; he was too busy for play at baseball and football, which seemed to him no more interesting than "pussy wants a corner." He had a workshop and spent every spare minute there. (He had begun working with wood and sharp tools at the age of four.) He made clock cases, bread boards, and picture frames, turning them out on his jig saw or his lathe: and built up quite a trade of his own. Evenings were spent drawing and designing articles to be made in the shop. "I should like a job as a lighthouse tender," he says, "where the supply boat came only once every three months. I might have enough uninterrupted time to get something done."

His inventive capacity was demonstrated when a test oil-well was made on his father's land. The oil driller dropped his tools when he was down some fifteen hundred feet. He complained that he could not recover the tools. "She's down more'n fifteen hunnerd feet; 'n' the bottom fi' hunnerd feet is plugged full o' rope; ol' rotten, wet, sand-soaked rope rammed down like er wad in a gun. Nippin' tools ain't no good. 'Tain't no use wastin' time tryin' to get them out. Better start a new hole some'eres near."

Chev was listening and thinking. The word impossible intrigued him. There was power enough, he knew; he had seen the rope pull up the half ton of drilling tools many times. A new tool would have to be perfected. He got his pencil and sketched a harpoon that could be screwed into the lower rod of the jar mechanism in place of the drill bit. The old driller grinned, "Idea's all right, but ye can't make no sech tool." The boy went to a forge in Pittsburgh and came back with his harpoon. The tool worked. The well was completed, but it was a "duster."

One day he heard his mother ask a man who was working in the garden to remove the pushed-in cork from an olive oil bottle. "It can't be done, missus," was his reply. His mother wanted to use the bottle. So she went to Chev.

He had got the rope plug out of the oil well. "I shall ask him about this cork," she said. The boy set to work to invent a wire loop tool. In a short time he fished out the troublesome cork. These two cases of extracting foreign bodies were indicative of his future career.

Graduating from the Greentree Township school, Chevalier passed the entrance examinations and entered the University of Pittsburgh. He completed the pre-medical course and spent a year under the preceptorship of a Pittsburgh physician. In 1884 he was ready academically to enter medical school, but he was still struggling with poverty. His father's efforts to run a country hotel had met with failure; and he was now practically bankrupt. Chevalier had been working in a glass decorator's shop, painting china.

After he had paid his tuition at Jefferson Medical College in Philadelphia, he had left only sixty-three cents a day with which to meet all expenses for the collegiate term of six months. He found an attic room for one dollar a week. He was given his supply of coal in return for carrying fuel to the other eight rooms in the house. The four-flight climb was a wind-developer that substituted for sports. He did his own cooking, and soon became adept at concocting dishes for himself and his fellow students on the third floor. The day began at four-thirty with a creamless cup of coffee and butterless butt of bread, followed by study until nine. The morning coal was carried and then lectures began. Lunch consisted of an apple and two pretzels. Lectures closed at six. While dinner was boiling the night coal was carried. Evenings were devoted to study.

He spent the summer selling medical books to doctors in New England. Having covered his allotted territory, he found himself in Gloucester, Massachusetts. He had sent home sixty dollars to be saved for medical school expenses and had accumulated credit to buy a good supply of medical books. "My clothes," he writes, "were threadbare, my only remaining shirt on my back. My shoe soles were worn through; there were holes in the toes. A piece cut out of each shoe tongue and inserted inside the respective toe holes, with a stitch each side for anchorage, prevented protrusion of darned socks. An insole cut from pasteboard fresh each day or two prevented wearing away of the socks at the holes worn through in the soles of the shoes. And always the shoes were cleaned and polished with the brush I carried in my bag. The tools in the 'ditty bag' did good service in turning under frayed trousers. Not only socks were darned, but the seat of the trousers had several areas of basket weaving. Any skilful needlewoman would have pronounced it good work; there was no clumsy needlework to be ashamed of, but the shelter from public view given by the rather long coats then in fashion helped maintain an air of respectability. The worn-out and darned elbows were not so easily concealed; but hiding them was accomplished by keeping the palms turned forward. I always tried to appear fresh and clean, face, hands, and piccadilly collar of glistening celluloid washed often; and the pocket comb was used at every opportunity. But there is an end to all things—especially fabrics; and I was a shabby-genteel, threadbare, down-at-the-heel remnant of a book agent, gaunt and often weak from cutting too close on the food supply."

He signed up with a codfish boat starting for the Grand Banks. The cook fell sick and he took over the job, winning the favor of the crew with his coffee and the new dishes that he managed to create in the tiny galley. There was more work in the decorating shop, and then at last return to medical school, to the attic, to the coal hoppers, and the fascination of the operating room. On a spring evening in 1886 a jubilant crowd assembled to see the medical degrees awarded. The home folks cheered as the candidates mounted the stage to receive their diplomas. When the name Chevalier Jackson was called there was silence. The young man walked up the steps with an ache in his heart. His parents were too desperately poor to come to his graduation. The silence was so distressing that a kindly, old lady clapped her hands feebly.

The boyish doctor arrived home with the same short coat and cap that he had worn away to college. Under his arm was a diploma in a green tin tubular box. He was determined to become a specialist in the diseases of the nose and throat. It was a new field, a precarious adventure. It was necessary to go abroad to see what was being done by a pioneer such as Sir Morrell Mackenzie. He saved what he could from his few miserable fees, and made something painting glass. And then came a windfall. An eccentric old bachelor offered him fifty dollars toward his trip if he would obtain the latest information on the treatment of his chronic laryngeal ailment, and agree to take care of him for the balance of his life.

He crossed steerage on a twelve-hundred-ton Dutch steamer, caring for the steerage patients during their seasickness and taking charge of a smallpox epidemic. He made good use of his stay in London, and arrived in Pittsburgh with one dollar and seventy-six cents remaining; and set to work to open his office. Fellow doctors discouraged him. "You'll never make a living as a specialist," they said. The first twelve years of his practice were a struggle with poverty. He was busy working sixteen hours a day, but most of his practice was among the poor. He lived from hand to mouth, limiting his expenses in the strictest fashion. He gave freely of his energy in the slums, alleys, and hospital wards of the city. He discovered that thousands of children in the schools were suffering with infected tonsils. He showed the school board how these apathetic, sickly children could be transformed through the operation of tonsillectomy. They urged him to take it to the politicians. He began in his own district, which was known as the "bloody third" ward. Political bosses sidetracked him. They were interested in graft, not children. Dr. Jackson determined to fight for the welfare of the youth of Pittsburgh. As a result he was overwhelmed with charity work when he could not pay his own bills.

A born designer and inventor, he would work in his shop at night to perfect new instruments for his surgical work. He had seen an impractical device in London that was used to inspect the esophagus—the passage from the mouth to the stomach. In 1890 he developed an esophagoscope with which he removed a tooth-plate from the esophagus of an adult and a coin from that of a child. The development of this instrument brought a long line of sad cases, especially stricture of the esophagus from swallowing of lye. Children would pick up lye in the kitchen, and eat it, thinking it was sugar. Scalded and burned, their throats would close up, and they would die of thirst and starvation.

"One day a little girl seven years old, emaciated to a skeleton, arrived with the message she had not been able to swallow a drop of water for a week," relates Dr. Jackson. "She looked wistfully at a glass of water. Then she tried to swallow some of it, choked, coughed—and all the water came back through the nose and mouth. The two Sisters of Mercy said they had found the child lying on the floor of a coal miner's shanty, where they had gone to see the mother, who was dying of pneumonia. The father was lying on the floor in a drunken stupor. The little girl's ragged dirty clothing was soaking-wet. She was crying for water, and a three-year-old brother was supplying it with a tin cup from a tin pail. But evidently the water had run out of her mouth and soaked her clothing, because she could not swallow it. I put down the esophagoscope between her dry parched lips and found a tight stricture of the esophagus.

The scars had not completely closed the passage; in its narrowest part was a cork-like plug of grayish material. I removed the plug with delicate forceps passed through the esophagoscope.

"After removal of the instrument the child was given a glass of water. She took a small sip expecting it to choke her and come back up. It went slowly down; she took another sip, and it went down. Then she gently moved aside the glass of water in the nurse's hand, and took hold of my hand, and kissed it. She took more water and a glass of milk. The nurse put the child to bed, and coming back reported: 'She dropped off to sleep. It will be a wonder if she lives: she is just skin and bones.' She did live. When she got stronger the Sisters had her admitted to a Catholic orphanage and brought her in regularly for treatment. With the esophagoscope the stricture was dilated until at the end of two years she could swallow any kind of food in a perfectly normal way; and she grew well and strong.

"No money could give satisfaction equal to that of such an achievement. That wan smile and kiss of the hand from the grateful child whose swallowing was restored after a week of water starvation meant more to me than any material remuneration; the memory of it now, over forty years later, still yields dividends of satisfaction."

There were scores of cases of lye poisoning that passed under his hands. His heart was touched by this needless suffering. He lay awake wondering what he could do to save these children. He determined that two things must be done: a warning label must be put on containers; and a nation-wide campaign of education inaugurated so that these caustic poisons would be kept out of the reach of children. He went to the packers of lye-containing preparations. They discouraged him. "No such thing as a poison label can be put on my product unless it is put on every other; otherwise no one would buy mine. Suppose you got the packers to agree; new concerns would be coming out all the time. It is impossible to regulate it."

He went to the politicians; and they told him that it was impossible to put through a reform unless some philanthropist was willing to spend a fortune on it. He had heard the word impossible before, and was determined to keep on. He would gather scientific data to prove the curse of lye poisoning; he would write, speak, and agitate, and keep up the fight.

The esophagoscope led to the development of the bronchoscope, which was used for examining and treating the bronchi and the lungs, and for extracting foreign bodies. He made thousands of experiments on dogs in order to perfect the instrument and develop his technique. Countless lives were saved by his skilful use of this new instrument as he extracted nails, pins, buttons, jewelry, coins, bones, and other foreign objects from the lungs of children and adults, who were faced with certain death without the relief which he was able to give.

One of many dramatic cases is the story of a boy who came from Australia with a nail in his lung. Dr. Jackson removed the nail and made no charge. The Department of State, many organizations, and individuals expressed their thanks. After the boy's return to his home country five thousand school children gathered for a ceremony as the lad planted a tree in honor of his friend, Chevalier Jackson. It was characteristic of the surgeon who never cared for money and was always interested in humanity. As he once put it: "No hospital has ever paid me one cent, nor even reimbursed me for the thousands of dollars I have been spending in serving hospitals. Even the instruments I used, I had to buy myself for many years. For nearly fifty years I have been teaching in medical colleges. Not one cent of salary has any medical school ever paid me for my work, nor has any reimbursed me for my expenditures.

Many a time after saving a child's life I have given the parents money to pay their expenses home. Never once during this fifty years has any patient applying to me been refused treatment because of inability to pay."

He did not think of bronchoscopy as a means for increasing his income. He was eager to pass on his secret to other surgeons and to disseminate what he had learned. He gave bronchoscopic courses in Pittsburgh, Philadelphia, Paris; was invited to lecture in many parts of the world, and to establish new chairs in many medical schools. Each time his mother saw him she would say, "Teach everything you know to everyone who will listen." The expense of these trips was a heavy drain on his limited income. He kept his engagements with difficulty, because the money for his round-trip ticket was often hard to find. He went to cheap lodgings, ate a ten-cent breakfast, with his apple and pretzels for lunch, and soup and bread for supper. His distinguished listeners did not realize the sacrifice that he was making.

In 1911 a medical friend examined Jackson because of a troublesome cough; and announced that he had tuberculosis. He was just beginning to establish himself and to provide adequately for his wife and son. It was a heavy blow! He must follow a strict routine: twelve hours each day in bed and a rigid diet. After six months the disease was arrested; and he returned to practice for two years. Then one evening at a medical meeting he had a sudden hemorrhage. This time he went to a house in the country and to an enforced rest. The second attack seemed a dire calamity, but it gave him the chance to write his book, *Peroral Endoscopy and Laryngeal Surgery,* to gather together invaluable data that he had collected, and to make his own sketches.

The understanding of his wife and his happy home were factors in his recovery. "Countless times I have arrived home so weak I did not believe I should live through the night," he has said, "nor, if surviving, that I could return to work the next morning. But my home was always to me, metaphorically speaking, what a charging plant is to a storage battery. I came home exhausted. The restful quiet and sympathy charged me with energy so that I could leave the next morning with stored power to get through the troubles, anxieties, and difficulties of the day at the clinic. Every evening I entered a sanctuary; each morning I left refilled with courage."

At the age of thirty-five Dr. Jackson was made a professor of medicine in what is now the University of Pittsburgh. He was soon serving on the staff of fourteen Pittsburgh hospitals. The New York Post-Graduate Medical School and Hospital elected him professor of bronchoscopy and had him organize the new department in 1915. Called to become professor of laryngology at Jefferson Medical College, he moved to Philadelphia in 1916. He became professor in four other medical schools besides carrying on a busy practice. In the midst of his creative work came the third storm of tuberculosis. He purchased an old sawmill and gristmill in the country and here recovered his health. A fireproof study was built and all his valuable case records given a safe lodging. The out-of-doors encouraged him to write. His favorite writing post was in a boat on the mill pond.

His fight to protect children against lye was not yet won. He made many trips at his own expense to Washington, agitated at conferences and struggled to keep the problem before the American people. With the help of the American Medical Association he organized a committee with members from every state. Wide-spread publicity was undertaken to educate the people. State laws were enacted by twenty-four states. At last, in 1927, Congress passed the federal Caustic Act providing for a poison and antidote label. Victory had come after a battle of over twenty-five years.

The surgeon was now established as one of Philadelphia's most distinguished and honored citizens. It must have been a satisfaction to him to look back on the day when he gave his demonstration before the American Laryngological Association and successfully removed a price-tag from the lung of a stocking factory worker. Some had complimented him on his new instrument and its skilful use. But one famous surgeon, peeping into the porthole of the operating room, snorted, "damned nonsense!" He has lived to see his specialty recognized around the world.

Chevalier Jackson leads a very simple life. He goes to practically no social functions, eats no meat, uses neither tobacco nor alcohol. He is a great believer in work. He says, "Work with me is incessant. I do not remember a single day in the last thirty years getting up in the morning and asking myself, 'Well, what shall I do today?' Never once have I been free to choose what I might want to do. Each morning there has been laid out a list of things I *must* do whether I wanted to or not." From boyhood he trained himself to be ambidextrous in order to have both hands ready to carry his fertile ideas into action. He learned to saw, to write, to draw with his left hand. Today both hands are disciplined and skilful. His fingers received early schooling in twisting paper lighters for kindling lamps and fires, in painting, drawing, and woodworking. At seven he was doing Sorrento work; at ten, fine inlaying. He has always enjoyed sketching with chalk, painting in oils, and etching. He is able to illustrate his own books.

A layman once wrote rather indignantly to Dr. Jackson: "Will you please tell me what pleasure you have in life, if any? They say you do not smoke, drink, dine, dance, visit, fish, play bridge, golf, tennis, or any other game, go out or receive socially, go to baseball or football games, movies, plays or concerts; that you never travel or take an auto trip for pleasure and that you do not take a vacation."

Dr. Jackson has never been physically robust. Most of his life he has had to fight against impaired health. He is a small man, quiet and gentle in manner, friendly, and unaffected. But he has courage, a bulldog tenacity, and is a titan for work. The lure of the impossible has led him through the years. At seventy-five he smiles over the memory of Greentree school days. His tormentors smashed his sled, filled his boots with snow, smeared mud on his drawings, tied him up in the deserted mine, but they did not break his purpose. Small, frail, despised by the bullies, he kept faith in himself. Chicken-hearted, they called him, but he was to prove the conqueror of pain, the champion of childhood, a benefactor of humanity.

A Promise to Keep:

MARGARET SANGER

Tomatoes, apples, and cabbage stumps were flung about the meeting hall as Colonel Robert Ingersoll began his address in the little town of Corning, New York. The chairman of the meeting—a tall, red-headed Irishman named Michael Higgins—waved his arms and announced that they would adjourn from the hall and meet one hour later in the woods near by for the lecture. He walked out defiantly with the famous liberal at his side, his big fist clutching the hand of his little daughter, Margaret. Her head was held just as high as his, her eyes sparkled their challenge to the hooting crowd. For the first time this brave child of a rebel father was to feel the disdain of the mob. It was not the last time, however. From that day Margaret and her brothers and sister were known as children of the devil. On the way to school names were shouted at them, tongues stuck out, grimaces made. They were branded as heretics.

Michael Higgins was a stonecutter and depended for the support of his wife and eleven children upon the monuments he made for the cemetery. The local priest was incensed over the Ingersoll lecture, which had been staged under subterfuge in the hall that he owned. After that there were no more marble angels to be carved for the cemetery, and income was materially lessened. There were days of poverty and struggle for the family, but the rebel-idealist father refused to compromise on his advanced ideas. He insisted that the Christian religion should be put into practice, that his children's duty did not lie in considering what might happen to them after death, but in doing something here and now to make the lives of other human beings more decent. "You have no right to material comforts," he said, "without giving back to society the benefit of your honest experience. Leave the world better because you have dwelt in it."

Margaret was as strong-willed and courageous as her father. She tells how, as a child, she mastered her fears. "I began to make myself do the things I dreaded most to do—to go upstairs alone to bed without a light, to go down into the cellar without singing, to get up on the rafters in the barn and jump down on the hay stack thirty or forty feet below. When I had conquered all these dreaded fears, I felt more secure and stronger within myself. There was, however, one thing I dreaded more than anything in life. It was to walk on the ties of the railroad bridge which spanned the Chemung River. Two or three years before I had been taken across the iron structure by my father and brother, who often went there to fish in the river below. I had been held by both hands as I made those steps and looked down from the dizzy heights into the water. We had friends across the river on a large luxurious farm, but to get there we usually walked three miles in a roundabout way across another wooden bridge for traffic and pedestrians. I could not recall the experience of that perilous walk with my father and brother without feeling dizzy or faint.

"Now, however, as I began to strengthen my weaker 'me,' I decided that this walk must be taken—and alone. We were forbidden ever to go near that part of the town without an older member of the family. Nevertheless, I felt I must walk across that bridge. I trembled with fear as I got near the place, but the more afraid I felt the more determined I was to make myself do it. There was no turning back once I started across. I did not know the schedule of the trains, but I did remember which was the side for the up trains and which for the down trains. I can recall now how stolidly I put that left foot on the first tie; and with head up I started the venturesome walk which would make me faint if I tried it today. I dared not look down at the water; I wanted terribly to see that my foot was placed firmly on the tie, but could not trust my head, so I kept on.

"When about a quarter of the way across, I heard the singing of the steel rails! I knew a train was speeding towards me! I could not see it because a curve in the road was just beyond the end of the bridge. The singing grew stronger, and I crossed on one tie to the iron bars, deciding to hold fast there until the train went past, but suddenly around the curve the huge engine emerged, snorting, whistling like a cruel angry monster. It came so quickly that I tried to hide behind the iron girder to protect myself from the force of the speed, when my foot slipped and I fell through the space, saved only by the fact that both arms had not been able to pass through; and there I was, left dangling on that bridge while the five-car passenger train of the Erie went rushing past. All I thought of at the time was the hope that the engineer would not emit the sizzling steam as I had seen it done time after time when the trains whizzed past us at the station. I bowed my head, shut my eyes, and prayed to the engineer not to emit the steam. I was thankful when the train passed, but realized I was helpless to get up, as there was nothing to support my feet. There I hung, I do not know how long, until my terror subsided at the sight of a man, a friend of my father's, who was fishing on the bridge and who came to my rescue and pulled the fat, aching little body out of the hole. He gave me a scolding and asked if my father knew I was over there. He tried to set me toward home, advising me to go straight back.

"I knew I never could go back home defeated. It was just as impossible to go back instead of forward as it was to stop breathing. Terrified though I was, and bruised and bleeding as well, the remainder of that journey across the bridge was somehow easier than the first part. When I stepped off the bridge I ran happily to the farm to see our friends, and yet refrained from telling them of the journey lest I get another scolding.

"After this, I felt almost grown up. I did not talk about it, but something inside me had conquered something else."

Her mother, a pretty, slender woman, of Irish lineage since the days of the Norman Conquest, was a lover of beauty. The house was never without flowers, although there was no money to spend for such luxuries. She made the woods and fields her garden. She always had a cough, and was frail, but the flame of unfaltering courage never dimmed in her gray eyes. She was loyal to her impractical, dreamer husband and devoted to her eleven children.

Margaret's eighth-grade teacher, a cantankerous and sarcastic woman, aroused her independent spirit. One morning in mid-June the girl reached school two minutes late. Her tardiness was caused by taking too long to admire her first pair of kid gloves, which her sister had given her. The teacher delighted in making an example of her. "Well, Miss Higgins, so your ladyship has arrived at last! Ah, a new pair of gloves! I wonder that she even deigns to come to school at all."

There were giggles and titters. Margaret prayed that the woman would stop. But she did not. She kept on tormenting the girl. Margaret jerked her books from the desk and whisked out of the room. She rushed home to her mother. "I will never go back to that school again! I have finished forever. I'll go to jail, I'll work, I'll starve, I'll die! But back to that school and teacher I will never go!"

Parents, brothers, and sisters endeavored to persuade her, but she was adamant. It was only two weeks before the end of the school year, but her will could not be broken. In desperation they sent her for two weeks to Chautauqua to hear music and lectures, hoping to win her back to the routine of education. She was enrolled at Claverack, in the Catskill Mountains, where the Methodist farmers sent their children. One sister paid her tuition and the other bought her books and clothes. She washed dishes and waited on table to meet the balance of her expenses.

Her career as a teacher began some years later in the first grade of a New Jersey school with eighty-four pupils, the majority of whom could not speak English. Then she was summoned home to nurse her mother, who was dying with tuberculosis. The invalid was kept in an air-tight room, with doors and windows shut. Margaret borrowed books from the local doctor to read up on tuberculosis. One day she announced to him that she was going to study medicine. He smiled tolerantly, "You'll get over it." After her mother's death she took over the household responsibilities, buying the food, cooking, cleaning, mending, managing the finances. But she did not forget her goal.

As soon as she could arrange it, she entered a hospital as a student nurse. It was a rigorous training. There were no elevators, no electric lights or bells, and no interne physicians to advise and guide the nurses in the routine care of patients. The hospital was poorly equipped, and the nurses were compelled to do all kinds of drudgery. But she liked the work; it was her calling; she was now accomplishing something for humanity. At one of the hospital dances her doctor partner introduced her to a young architect named William Sanger, who was helping him build his home. The nurse and the architect were aware of the sudden electric quality in the atmosphere.

Next morning, when Margaret went out of the door for her customary walk she found William Sanger on the doorstep. The romantic gesture appealed to her. He had been waiting all night for her. At the end of her training period, they were married.

A few months later she fell ill with the same disease that had afflicted her mother. She was sent to Dr. Trudeau's sanitarium at Saranac. It was a gloomy atmosphere, a depressing place for a young wife who was expecting her first baby. She went to New York for the birth of her son Stuart, and then took the baby back with her to a small Adirondack village. She tried to keep up the treatment given at Trudeau's sanitarium: creosote capsules, plenty of food and rest.

At the end of eight months she was worse instead of better. Two of Dr. Trudeau's associates urged her to go to Saranac and to give up all family responsibility.

"What would you like to do with yourself?" they asked.

"Nothing," she answered.

"Where would you like to go?"

"Nowhere."

"Would you like to have the baby sent to your brother, or would you rather have your mother-in-law take it?"

"I don't care."

She was indifferent to every suggestion. She had lost the will to live.

One of the doctors returned later, laid his hand on her shoulder, and urged, "Don't be like this! Don't let yourself get into such a mental condition. Do something! Want something! You'll never get well if you keep on this way!"

She could not shake off the doctor's challenge. What would she do? Give up to her lingering illness and prepare to die? Or would she recapture her dream of living for humanity? She got up at five o'clock in the morning and announced that she was going home. Her confused husband met her at Grand Central Station. He had received two telegrams; one stating that she was being removed to Saranac at once, and the other that she was returning to New York. He comforted her, "You did just the right thing. I won't let you die."

She soon recovered her desire for food and her interest in life. The old-time resolution reasserted itself, the will to live returned, and she won her way back to health. There followed many idyllic days in a new suburban home. When later the attractive house was burned, she took it philosophically, saying, "It was as though a chapter of my life had been brought to a close, and I was neither disappointed nor regretful. On the contrary, I was conscious of a certain relief, of a burden lifted. In that instant I learned the lesson of the futility of material substances. Of what great importance were they spiritually if they could go so quickly? Pain, thirsts, heartaches could be put into the creation of something external, which in one sweep could be taken from you. With the destruction of the house, my scale of suburban values was consumed. I could never again pin my faith on concrete things; I must build on myself alone. I hoped I should continue to have lovely objects around me, but I could also be happy without them!"

A second son was born, and a daughter followed to fill happy days with action. But the busy mother felt, as she expressed it, "a discontent with the futility of my present course. After my experience as a nurse with fundamentals this quiet withdrawal into the tame domesticity of the pretty riverside settlement seemed to be bordering on stagnation. I felt as though we had drifted into a swamp, but we would not wait for the tide to set us free." She would return to nursing.

Trained nurses were in demand, and she took many obstetrical cases. There were numerous calls to the lower East Side of New York. She was drawn there magnetically by a force outside her control. She hated the wretchedness and hopelessness of the poor. The poverty of families she helped and the uncertain future of their children tormented her.

"The utmost depression came over me as I approached this region. Below Fourteenth Street I seemed to be breathing a different air, to be in another world and country where the people had habits and customs alien to anything I had ever heard about.

"There were then approximately ten thousand apartments in New York into which no sun ray penetrated directly; such windows as they had opened only on a narrow court from which rose fetid odors. It was seldom cleaned, though garbage and refuse often went down into it. All these dwellings were pervaded by the foul breath of poverty, that moldy, indefinable, indescribable smell which cannot be fumigated out, sickening to me but apparently unnoticed by those who lived there. When I set to work with antiseptics, their pungent sting, at least temporarily, obscured the stench.

"I remember one confinement case to which I was called by the doctor of an insurance company. I climbed up the five flights of stairs and entered the airless rooms, but the baby had come with too great speed. A boy of ten had been the only assistant. Five flights was a long way; he had wrapped the placenta in a piece of newspaper and dropped it out the window into the court.

"Each time I returned to this district, which was becoming a recurrent nightmare, I used to hear that Mrs. Cohen 'had been carried to a hospital, but had never come back,' or that Mrs. Kelly 'had sent the children to a neighbor and had put her head into the gas oven.' There were abortions, deaths, suicides because of the continual stream of unwanted children, children who could not be fed, who were destined to live in prisons of poverty and ignorance. Day after day such tales were poured into my ears—a baby born dead, great relief—the death of an older child, sorrow but again relief of a sort—the story told a thousand times of death from abortion and children going into institutions. I shuddered with horror as I listened to the details and studied the reasons back of them—destitution linked with excessive childbearing. The waste of life seemed utterly senseless. One by one worried, sad, pensive, and aging faces marshaled themselves before me in my dreams, sometimes appealingly, sometimes accusingly.

"These were not merely 'unfortunate conditions among the poor' such as we read about. I knew the women personally. They were living, breathing, human beings, with hopes, fears, and aspirations like my own, yet their weary, misshapen bodies, 'always ailing, never failing' were destined to be thrown on the scrap heap before they were thirty-five. I could not escape from the facts of their wretchedness; neither was I able to see any way out. My own cozy and comfortable family existence was becoming a reproach to me."

One summer night she was called to a Grand Street tenement to the bedside of a Jewish mother twenty-eight years old. The hot crowded apartment was in turmoil. Jake Sachs, a truck driver, was trying to care for three crying babies and his wife, who was desperately ill with blood poisoning after she had lost a child prematurely. It was a stiff battle for a fortnight in an inferno of heat, where water, ice, drugs, and food had to be carried up three flights of stairs. Mrs. Sanger went home exhausted, but with the satisfaction of knowing that she had saved another life.

A few months later the telephone rang. It was Jake Sachs' troubled voice announcing that his wife was sick again and from the same cause. This was to prove a momentous night in Margaret Sanger's life, as her own words record.

"For a wild moment I thought of sending someone else, but actually, of course, I hurried into my uniform, caught up my bag, and started out. All the way I longed for a subway wreck, an explosion, anything to keep me from having to enter that home again. But nothing happened, even to delay me. I turned into the dingy doorway and climbed the familiar stairs once more. The children were there, young little things.

"Mrs. Sachs was in a coma and died within ten minutes. I folded her still hands across her breast, remembering how she had pleaded with me, begging so humbly for the knowledge which was her right. I drew a sheet over her pallid face. Jake was sobbing, running his hands through his hair and pulling it out like an insane person. Over and over again he wailed, 'My God! My God! My God!'

"I left him pacing desperately back and forth, and for hours I myself walked and walked and walked through the hushed streets. When I finally arrived home and let myself quietly in, all the household was sleeping. I looked out my window and down upon the dimly lighted city. Its pains and griefs crowded in upon me, a moving picture rolled before my eyes with photographic clearness: women writhing in travail to bring forth little babies; the babies themselves naked and hungry, wrapped in newspapers to keep them from the cold; six-year-old children with pinched, pale, wrinkled faces, old in concentrated wretchedness, pushed into gray and fetid cellars, crouching on stone floors, their small scrawny hands scuttling through rags, making lamp shades, artificial flowers; white coffins, black coffins, coffins, coffins interminably passing in never-ending succession. The scenes piled one upon another on another. I could bear it no longer.

"As I stood there the darkness faded. The sun came up and threw its reflection over the house tops. It was the dawn of a new day in my life also. The doubt and questioning, the experimenting and trying, were now to be put behind me. I knew I could not go back merely to keep people alive.

"I went to bed, knowing that no matter what it might cost, I was finished with palliatives and superficial cures; I was resolved to seek out the root of evil, to do something to change the destiny of mothers whose miseries were vast as the sky!"

With her sacred promise to keep, Margaret Sanger set out to study in medical centers and libraries, to travel in England, France, Germany, Holland—seeking for facts that she could give to the burdened, driven masses of the world. A way must be found whereby families could be limited: a technique for birth control.

In 1914 she started the *Woman Rebel* to carry her crusade among the women of America. She was editor, manager, circulation department, bookkeeper, and paid the bills. The Post Office Department advised her that the magazine was unmailable under the postal laws and regulations. She must choose between abandoning the *Woman Rebel* or make herself liable to a Federal indictment and a possible prison term of five years plus a fine of five thousand dollars. She determined to continue. The magazine brought amazing results. Within six months ten thousand letters were received from all over the world requesting knowledge about birth control. Her family pleaded with her to give up this dangerous task of liberalism. She had outdistanced even her rebel father. The family sent him to New York to try to persuade her to go to a sanitarium for a rest. But she held resolutely to her course.

The Post Office Department arraigned her for trial, and there was wide-spread discussion in the press. Sympathy was for her cause. The unreasonable and inhuman postal laws were condemned. After a brief hearing, her trial was postponed until autumn. As the date drew near, friends convinced her of the wisdom of going abroad rather than face certain imprisonment and fine. She reasoned, "I was not afraid of the penitentiary; I was not afraid of anything except being misunderstood. Nevertheless, in the circumstances, my going there could help nobody. I had seen so many people do foolish things valiantly, such as wave a red flag, shout inflammatory words, lead a parade, just for the excitement of doing what the crowd expected of them. Then they went to jail for six months, a year perhaps, and what happened? Something had been killed in them; they were never heard of again. I had seen braver and hardier souls than I vanquished in spirit and body by prison terms, and I was not going to be lost and broken for an issue which was not the real one, such as the entirely unimportant *Woman Rebel* articles. Had I been able to print *Family Limitation* earlier, and to swing the indictment around that, going to jail might have had some significance.

"Going away was much more difficult than remaining. But if I were to sail for Europe I could prepare my case adequately and return then to win or lose in the courts. There was a train for Canada within a few hours. Could I take it? Should I take it? Could I ever make those who had advised me against this work and these activities understand? How could I separate myself from the children without seeing them once more? Peggy's leg was swollen from vaccination. This kept worrying me, made me hesitate, anxious. It was so hard to decide what to do.

"Perfectly still, my watch on the table, I marked the minutes fly. There could be no retreat once I boarded that train. The torture of uncertainty, the agony of making a decision only to reverse it! The hour grew later and later. This was like both birth and death—you had to meet them alone.

"About thirty minutes before train time I knew that I must go. I wrote two letters, one to Judge Hazel, one to Attorney Content, to be received at the desk the next day, informing them of my action. I had asked for a month and it had been refused. This denial of right and freedom compelled me to leave my home and my three children until I made ready my case, which dealt with society rather than an individual. I would notify them when I came back. Whether this were in a month or a year depended on what I found it necessary to do. Finally, as though to say, 'Make the most of it,' I enclosed to each a copy of *Family Limitation*.

"Parting from all that I held dear in life, I left New York at midnight, without a passport, not knowing whether I could ever return."

She journeyed again to England, and there she was reassured by such liberals as Dr. and Mrs. C. V. Drysdale (of the Neo-Malthusian Society), Edward Carpenter, and Havelock Ellis (whom she calls one of the greatest minds she ever met). In Holland she met Dr. Johannes Rutgers, a pioneer woman physician, who convinced her that clinics were the proper place for dissemination of birth control. There followed travel and study in France and Spain, and then return to the United States to continue the fight. A few days after her homecoming her daughter, Peggy, fell ill with pneumonia and died. Friends from all over America sent sympathy and contributions for her forthcoming trial. Marie Stopes, H. G. Wells, and other liberals addressed a letter to President Woodrow Wilson pointing out the fact that Margaret Sanger was in danger of criminal prosecution for circulating a pamphlet on birth control, which was allowed in every civilized country except the United States, and that to suppress serious and disinterested opinion on anything so important was detrimental to human progress.

The Government stated that the indictment was two years old, that Mrs. Sanger was not a disorderly person, and dismissed the case. Immediately, the released crusader set out on a lecture tour across the country. When asked how long it took her to prepare that first lecture, she answered, "Fourteen years." She had spent many hours practising on the roof of the Lexington Avenue hotel, where she was staying, her voice echoing among the chimney pots.

When she arrived at the Victoria Theater in St. Louis to give her address, she found the building locked and in total darkness. The manager had been threatened with a boycott of his theater if he permitted the birth-control meeting. Two thousand people outside the theater were shouting, "Break in the door." Mrs. Sanger was urged to speak to the crowd from an automobile. As she began, a police sergeant gripped her by the arm and cried, "You can't speak here!" The Men's City Club asked her to speak at their luncheon the next day. Forty members resigned in a body, but more than one hundred new members joined to take their place. The press was stirred and made an appeal for freedom of speech. And so it was across the continent; there was criticism and opposition, but everywhere came response and progress for the cause.

In 1916 Mrs. Sanger opened in New York City the first birth-control clinic in America. Arriving at the clinic early that historic morning, she saw the women waiting. "Halfway to the corner they were standing in line, at least one hundred and fifty, some shawled, some hatless, their red hands clasping the cold, chapped, smaller ones of their children." At seven in the evening they were still coming. "All were confused, groping among the ignorant sex-teachings of the poor, fumbling without guidance after truth, misled, and bewildered in a tangled jungle of popular superstitions and old wives' remedies. Unconsciously they dramatized the terrible need of intelligent and scientific instruction in these matters of life—and death."

It was only a matter of a short time before police entered the clinic, seized its records, and clamped Mrs. Sanger into the Raymond Street Jail, where she spent the night with roaches and rats, amid the stench and grime. At her trial she was sentenced to thirty days in the workhouse for giving out birth-control information, which was forbidden by state law. The days she spent in the Queens Penitentiary made a deep impression on her. She saw what the prison system was, how it affected human beings, what crime did to women, how the criminal derelicts of modern civilization lived. The cold spring morning that she stepped outside the metal doors a little group of her friends were gathered to celebrate her "coming-out party." They lifted their voices in song, and the women from the prison joined with them in words of the *Marseillaise:* "Ye sons of freedom, wake to glory!"

She had a promise to keep. There must be education, organization, and legislation. The cause must be won! Once again the busy routine: parlor meetings by day, open forums at night—from which she returned too tired and too excited to sleep. There was a trip to England and Europe. In post-war Germany she saw emaciated mothers who had nursed their babies for more than two years in the effort to save them from starvation. She heard countless stories from mothers who had been tortured by watching their children starve to death—"pinched faces growing paler, eyes more listless, heads drooping lower day by day until finally they did not even ask for food. You saw a tiny thing playing on the street suddenly run to a tree or fence and lean against it while he coughed and had a hemorrhage." She realized that her promise was made not only for Mrs. Jake Sachs and the mothers of the East Side in New York, it was for the sake of the mothers of the whole world!

The First National Birth Control Conference was held, the American Birth Control League was launched, articles and books were written, numberless addresses were given, and public meetings were staged—all for the purpose of awakening the people. There was continuous opposition. There were long, eventful trips to Japan, China, India, Russia, and England, where Mrs. Sanger met social liberals and carried her message to millions of people. Clinics were opened in the United States, and performed an inestimable service to countless women. They would be raided and closed; their organizer would be threatened, ridiculed, and condemned. But in spite of prejudice the crusade went steadily forward. Protestant and Jewish religious groups began to recognize and commend her cause. Sentiment for change in the Federal law was fostered.

In 1931, Mrs. Sanger held a debate with Chief Justice Richard B. Russell of Georgia on the subject, "Should the Federal laws be changed?" The judge had eighteen children by two wives, and his opposition to birth control was a good advertisement for its success. His opponent enjoyed the debate, as her description records: "The old judge, white-haired and with white eyebrows and mustache, his figure still erect, fixed me with a glance, sometimes satiric and sometimes flaming with the rage of an Old Testament prophet." He talked of the sacredness of motherhood, the home, and the State of Georgia: 'We don't need birth control in Georgia. We've had to give up two Congressmen now because we don't have enough people. If New York wants to wipe out her population, she can. We need ours. . . . I can take care of all the children God sent me. I believe God sent them to me because they have souls. Poodle dogs and jackasses don't have souls. I have obeyed the command of God to 'increase and multiply.'

"His children and their wives and their relatives occupying several rows of seats down front applauded vigorously."

Bills to repeal the archaic Federal law were brought before Congress. There were hearings. Enlightened leaders lent co-operation, but dogmatists reiterated the old arguments that have been used from the beginning of time to block human advancement: it was against the Bible, against God, against the country. She went to one Congressman, who was bitterly opposed to her bill, and tried to explain its purpose. She got nowhere with him. He was against birth control because of his religious prejudices. As she left his office he said, "You see, I'm just one of those unusual men who are very fond of children." I heard Mrs. Sanger repeat this story with a twinkle in her Irish eyes. "I came back at him and said, 'I love children as much as any parent on earth! I've had three of my own. You know as well as I do that you are begging the question!'"

She was continually misinterpreted and denounced as an enemy of the home, as a woman who despised motherhood, as a foe of children, when her sole object was the protection of the youth and the parents of the world.

The Congressional hearings met with defeat. In spite of the growing interest and enlightenment, public opinion was not yet ready to sustain a change in the Federal laws. It was a hard rebuff to meet rejection after years of sacrificial work and after thousands of dollars had been painfully raised and expended to bring the cause before Congress. It was a terrific burden to carry! But the cause could not be surrendered. The work must still go on: education, organization, legislation—until victory should come at last!

When I talked recently with Margaret Sanger I found her undaunted by the magnitude of the crusade. She is a charming woman, whose bright eyes shine with unconquerable hope. "Pioneering is not so difficult as some imagine. There have been many joys and rewards that have more than offset my few hardships. Every battle has been worth it. Of course, the struggle is far from being over. What freedom we have won must be safeguarded. But I have seen enough to believe that we are on the way to progress.

"The dictators of our time have set back the cause of woman. Everywhere they frown on liberation; they demand that woman shall be a slave of the state, content to produce good soldiers. In face of the bondage of fear and prejudice we can do nothing better than continue to contend for the freedom of human personality!"

In 1917, in the same Town Hall in New York where police had once forbidden her to speak, she received a medal of honor. Pearl Buck spoke for the women of the world when she said, "Because I am so convinced of the success of Margaret Sanger's cause, therefore, I am not going to talk about it today at all. I am not impatient as to the hour of final triumph. Inevitably as the sun rises, it is coming and coming quickly. In this generation it is tacitly accepted already, if still openly opposed by some few groups. In the next generation there will be no opposition, or opposition of so formal a kind as to be negligible.

"I give my honor to Margaret Sanger not chiefly because she has been the leader in a great movement for human progress, although it is the most important movement, I believe, in our times, and one which in the future will be understood to have contributed more than any other to our human race, not only economically, but intellectually and spiritually; I give her my honor for this, and for more. I honor her today for her fearless frankness, for proceeding in the face of prejudice to do what she saw to be right for people. No one has had a more difficult task than hers. No cause ever fought has been fought against more stupid blind social prejudice, not even the cause of the people against the divine rights of kings, nor the cause of equal suffrage, nor any of the battles for freedom."

The promise made by the young nurse that night in an East Side tenement has been kept!

SOURCES OF QUOTATIONS

The sources, other than interviews, letters, and news stories, of incidents and direct quotations included in this volume are listed below. The author is grateful to publishers of books who granted permission to use direct quotations.

CHARLES FRANKLIN KETTERING

"Boss Kettering," Paul de Kruif, *Saturday Evening Post.*
Research and Social Progress, Charles Kettering, General Motors Corporation.
Unfinished Business, Charles Kettering, General Motors Corporation.

RICHARD E. BYRD

Rear Admiral Byrd and the Polar Expedition, C. Foster, A. L. Burt & Co.
Exploring with Byrd, Richard E. Byrd, Putnam.
Little America, Richard E. Byrd, Putnam.
Discovery, Richard E. Byrd, Putnam.
Alone, Richard E. Byrd, Putnam.

EDOUARD BENEŠ

My War Memoirs, Edouard Beneš, Houghton Mifflin.

JAWAHARLAL NEHRU

The Autobiography of Jawaharlal Nehru, Jawaharlal Nehru, John Lane, The Bodley Head, Ltd.

LOUIS DEMBITZ BRANDEIS

Brandeis: The Personal Story of an American Ideal, Alfred Lief, Stackpole.

THOMAS MANN
Coming Victory of Democracy, Thomas Mann, Knopf.
This Peace, Thomas Mann, Knopf.
"The New Humanism," Thomas Mann, *Nation.*

MADAME CHIANG KAI-SHEK
Strong Man of China, Robert H. Berkov, Houghton Mifflin.
General Chiang Kai-shek, Chiang Kai-shek, Doubleday, Doran.
War Messages of Madame Chiang Kai-shek, Hankow, 1937.
Undated pamphlet published by the New Life Movement, Hankow.

CHEVALIER JACKSON
The Life of Chevalier Jackson, Chevalier Jackson, Macmillan.

MARGARET SANGER
An Autobiography, Margaret Sanger, Norton.
My Fight for Birth Control, Margaret Sanger, Farrar & Rinehart.